LA

A Land of
Magical Monasteries

Siân Pritchard-Jones
&
Bob Gibbons

ISBN: 978-1499515404

First published in 2006 by Pilgrims Publishing, Varanasi

Front cover photo: Thikse monastery
Back cover photo: Maitreya Buddha at Thikse monastery
Title page photo: Chemrey monastery
Text: Siân Pritchard-Jones and Bob Gibbons
Photos: Siân Pritchard-Jones and Bob Gibbons
Originally conceived by: Rama Tiwari and Joanne Stephenson
New edition design: Siân Pritchard-Jones and Bob Gibbons

Acknowledgements

Thanks to Rama Tiwari and Joanne Stephenson for asking us to write this book. The project greatly added to our fascination and knowledge of the incredible sights and overwhelmingly beautiful geographical settings of Ladakh.

To Ashish, Lala, Rhicha, Sunil, Arjun and the ever-patient staff of Pilgrims, who helped us to seek out the necessary information among the crowded bookshelves of the shop, deserve our thanks too. Thanks to Christopher for working flat out in Varanasi – the only position to be in!

Thanks to Bhandari's Photo Shop, Thamel, Kathmandu, for their prompt and efficient service.

In Leh we are grateful to M Yasin at the Hotel Lasermo, and Dorje Tsering at the Jigmet Guest House, for their hospitality, as well as the taxi drivers, in particular Mohamed Gul, who drove us over icy roads in the middle of winter to explore the hidden corners of the valleys.

Jet Airways provided the best in-flight omelette we have ever tasted!

Important note for the 2014 edition

Please note that the names of hotels and restaurants are likely to have changed considerably over the years, and as Ladakh has developed as a tourist destination there will almost certainly be far more choice than before.

The geography, history and location of the monasteries will not have changed; they have been there for centuries and continue to mesmerise and attract all visitors.

Please do contact us with your updates through our website **www.expeditionworld.com**. Thank you!

Authors' note

We apologise for any factual errors within the text. Many of the monasteries move their idols around from temple to temple, sometimes during renovations or for other unknown reasons. Some of the temples have been renamed over the past few years, some no longer exist and others are completely new. With regard to the strange and unpronounceable names of some of the idols, sometimes even the monks are not sure of the correct name, let alone transliteration. It would appear that statues, images and idols are periodically moved around within a chapel, or even to a different chapel, so this may also cause confusion.

It is a source of some regret that we have been unable to produce an exhaustive and complete guide to the many and varied monasteries of Ladakh, because of inclement weather and the unfortunate fact that on occasions the monk with the keys to some of the chapels have been 'in Leh' or otherwise engaged with pujas, death rites for the near-by deceased etc. What we have achieved is to list and describe the most accessible, convenient and most frequently visited monasteries closer to Leh. These have detailed maps and diagrams to aid identification of the numerous deities. By way of background we have also included details about many other monasteries of interest in Ladakh and Zanskar. Some of these we have visited in the past and some recently; some, however, we have not.

Having first visited Ladakh in 1977, we have seen many changes in the years since. Much of the research for this book was conducted in the winter of 2006. We have done our best to be as accurate as possible under the circumstances. Updates from Pilgrims and other sources are included where relevant. Sadly many copies of the original edition were lost in the fire that destroyed Pilgrims Book House in Kathmandu in May 2013, so we are bringing it back to the market through this CreateSpace publication.

Please do let us know if you discover any more hidden gems which we should include in future editions.

Ladakhi Road Signs

from Himank and the Border Roads Association

"Darling, I like you,
but not so fast"

"I am curvaceous,
be slow"

"Check your nerves
on my curves"

"Feel the curves,
do not test them"

"If married,
divorce speed"

"Don't find a fault,
find a remedy"

"The journey of life is long,
the path unknown"

"We cannot command nature,
except by obeying her"

"In the middle of difficulty,
find opportunity"

Contents

Preface

Knowledge is always purchased at the expense of what might have been seen and learned and was not...
Oppenheimer, Kathmandu Post

Ladakh is a land of magical mystery, where magnificent peaks reach to the heavens, and the depth of religious fervour in its mystical monasteries is unfathomable.

Ladakh is a harsh land; its bleak mountains offer few physical comforts to the traveller. In winter all is white; on a grey day the earth melts into the sky above, but on a sunny day the dazzling quality of the pristine snow standing dramatically against the deep blue sky is unforgettable. In summer the trees burst into life and greenery abounds, but the mountains are still majestic in their power and spirituality.

The Indus Valley around Leh in Ladakh has perhaps one of the greatest concentrations of monasteries anywhere in the world. This book will take you through these valleys, exploring the monasteries and hopefully adding further interest to your trip, whether as a trekker, sightseer or devoted pilgrim.

Come with us to this high-altitude fairyland; discover the fabulous architecture, exquisite arts, astonishing idols, quirky, whimsical imagery and enlightening vistas.

Bob Gibbons
Siân Pritchard-Jones
Kathmandu 2014

Introduction

When Ladakh first opened to tourism in the mid 1970s, no one could have predicted the amount of interest that its unique landscapes and culture would attract. In the early years of tourism to Ladakh, the lucky visitors were able to begin their sojourn from the enchanting Kashmir valley. After a short (or long) stay on the famous houseboats of Dal Lake in Srinagar, the traveller would head with some trepidation into the mountains. The only route to Leh was over the infamous, avalanche-prone Zoji La pass, following in the footsteps of famous explorers, missionaries and daredevil adventurers.

In the early 1980s, buses plied the tortuous road, taking two bone-shaking, at times heart-stopping days to reach Leh. On the way two very high passes would bar the way, the Namika La and the Fatu La, but the journey offered a myriad of landscapes. This was a rarely possible journey across the main Himalayan watershed. The lush, green forests of Kashmir gave way to the high altitude deserts of the barren, stark, near lifeless land and mountains of Ladakh.

After the mid 1980s, Kashmir was engulfed in security issues and a new route opened from Himachal Pradesh into the hidden kingdom. Today one can even visit (by air) in winter, and it is not altogether without charms at this time of year. Gone are the crowds, the people are more forthcoming, the monasteries are empty (even the monk with the key may not always be around!) That said, the snowy vistas and often luminescent clear blue skies offer a certain masochistic charm. At anything down to minus 35°C, cold it certainly can be, food is limited and, as for washing, your bucket of water may well turn to ice before you get your clothes off! Roads are usually open in the Indus valley, but excursions over to the Nubra valley or Pangong Lake may not be possible.

Whenever travelling to the high plateaux of western Tibet and Ladakh, the experience is sure to be one of visual overload. And as for tourism, today upwards of fifty thousand visitors descend on the mountain stronghold during the Hemis festival. Yet despite its growing popularity, Ladakh is a still a wonderland of cultural interest, of stark, captivating mountains, of fairytale, magical monasteries whose chapels are full of unworldly imagery.

Map of Ladakh

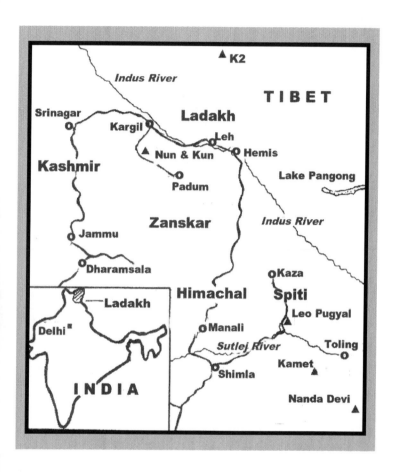

Chapter One

GEOGRAPHY OF LADAKH

We are looking upon the inexhaustibly rich rock formations. We note where and how were conceived the examples of symbolic images. Nature, having no outlet, inscribed epics with their wealth of ornamentation, on the rocks. One perceives how the forms of imagery blend with the mountain atmosphere.
Altai Himalaya: *Nicholas Roerich*

Ladakh is a high, mountainous land, consisting of many mountain peaks and ridges, twisted and bent by forces deep within the earth. The three main river valleys are the Indus, the Nubra and the Zanskar, which are so green and lush in summer yet so white and barren in winter. Truly a high altitude desert, it impresses on the mind just how insignificant we human beings are in comparison with the massive forces of nature. The two lakes of Pangong and Tshomo Riri also cut through this landscape of white or yellow – flashes of blue and green on an otherwise colourless canvas.

Ladakh is another world, beyond the wildest dreams of most people who have not had the chance to experience its exquisite and excruciating grandeur. From baking hot sunshine during the day, temperatures can drop to -40°C at night or even lower, chilling the spirit as well as the bone. But then the next morning a clear blue sky dispels all bad feelings; the sun warms the spirit as well as the body.

Midday temperatures in the summer sun can be higher than towns such as Delhi or Agra, though in the shade the temperatures are much lower. Even in winter the power of the sun is deceptively strong and liable to burn delicate human skin. As well as its intense heat and cold, Ladakh is also extremely dry, and its freezing dry air will parch the skin of anyone who goes outside unprotected.

Yet somehow, despite this unforgiving climate, Ladakh manages to produce some of the most delicious apricots of the region. The strong rays of the sun shining through the rarefied atmosphere enable several crops to grow during the short periods of summer, mainly barley.

Yaks, donkeys, wild horses, khyang (wild ass) and hares abound between 4900m and 5300m, while domestic and wild mountain goats survive and flourish even at heights above 5000m. The elusive and exquisite snow leopard is also found at high altitudes here, though you are unlikely to be lucky enough to see one.

Although there is practically no rain, snowfall provides sufficient water for these animals' survival. Meat and fruit can be dried and cured simply by placing them outside in this inhospitable land.

For over six months a year, road access to Ladakh is cut off by snow and the only access is by air, in a dramatic flight over some of the most beautiful mountains on earth.

Geological Events

The theory of plate tectonics has long been accepted as the principle reason why mountains have formed. According to this idea, huge surface plates 'float' on a mobile magma base and shift around over millions of years. The Himalaya and the Tibetan plateau were formed when the two plates of India and Tibet collided. Previously the area between these plates comprised the Tethys Sea. From abundant fossil records in Tibet and Nepal, it is estimated that this sea existed some one hundred million years ago.

Sometime in the next fifty million years, India began to run into Tibet and the first mountains were formed. These ranges are now the Kangtise, the Nyenchentangla north of Lhasa, and the Kunlun, which form the northern rim of the plateau. Some forty to forty-five million years ago, the Indian plate continued its northward march, forcing the plateau upwards. It currently folds under the Tibetan plate along the foothills of the Siwalik range that runs along the edge of the plains. Around 20 million years ago, the Himalaya were formed. The plateau region has risen further over the last two million years, as have the Himalaya.

Winds: In Yaglong, Nubra, June 1966

At about 3pm one day a devastating tornado blew through the whole area. A great many huts of the locals and a whole mule caravan carrying expensive loads to Baltistan was trapped in this tornado. To my amazement the mules, along with their loads, were literally lifted from the ground by the tornado and thrown away out of sight. Later I checked and found that they had been hurled a kilometre away and lay broken and dead from their strange aerial journey. The locals once again referred to the Jigbu and other evil spirits as being the cause of this most unusual happening. However further research indicated to me that such tornadoes are not all that rare as I had first thought they were.

from Ladakh the Wonderland by Brig. Teg Bahadur Kapur

Jigbu: the Ladakhi Yeti

The Jigbu is a mythical figure in Ladakhi culture, similar in many ways to the Nepalese yeti. He is said to be a giant man, who holds his breath for most of the day and night, but blows it out occasionally and explosively, causing violent and unexpected storms which appear out of nowhere.

Chapter Two

THE HISTORICAL PERSPECTIVE

The early history of Ladakh remains as much a mystery as the images and statues that its magnificent monasteries exhibit. In fact little detail is known about its history before the 7th century. One might imagine that the great caravans of Central Asia which passed this way all contributed to the culture, bringing outside influences to bear on the territory. The history of Ladakh has also been well integrated over thousands of years with events on the Tibetan plateau. Culturally it has closer links to Tibet than to India.

The Mon people are thought to have been some of the earliest inhabitants of Ladakh, possibly migrating by way of Kulu and Manali. Whether these people followed the Buddhist faith is not clear, but they are believed to have been well established across Ladakh before the 3rd century BC. Their main realm was centred on Zanskar, but it very likely spread across the region into Tibet.

The Dards are another fascinating group of people who migrated into Ladakh. Their descendants can still be found living along the banks of the Indus River in the villages of Domkhar and Skurbuchan, northwest of Khalatse and north of Dras. They probably came from Afghanistan and are thought to be descended from a particularly pure strain of the Aryans, who migrated to India possibly from the regions of Eastern Europe. The Dards were also believed to have settled in the area around Leh itself. The eminent author A. H. Francke, who explored Ladakh in the early 20th century, discovered what he thought were royal graves close to modern-day Leh. The Dards basically worshipped the elements – fire, earth, sun, moon, water, animals etc – and in this their ideas would have been close to the Bon of early Tibet, who also worshipped such phenomena.

The earliest Buddhists probably came to Ladakh in the 3rd century BC, but the religion did not become established for many more centuries. Whether Asoka, an early convert to Buddhism, visited or had influence in Ladakh is not known.

Perhaps one of the earliest influences appeared from the west in the form of the Ghandaran civilisation that emerged from northwest Pakistan. Taxila is one such centre in the region, near modern-day Rawalpindi. This predominantly Buddhist culture came first from India and Nepal and engulfed much of the subcontinent, as well as eastern Afghanistan, where the ancient Buddhas of Bamiyan were found. Buddhism spread all along the Silk Route well into China, and of course superseded the old Tibetan Bon faith on the plateau itself. There appear to be few Bon remnants in Ladakh now, although Lamayuru Monastery might once have belonged to the Bonpo.

In the 2nd century AD the Kushana Kings of the Kashmir region ruled over the predominantly Buddhist region that extended into Ladakh. King Kanishka is said to have constructed a chorten in Zanskar. As early as the 5th century AD, the cult of Maitreya Buddha appeared in Ladakh, according to the celebrated Chinese monk Fa Hsien. Prem Singh Jina, in his book 'Religious History of Ladakh', suggests that wooden Maitreya images were found in Sumda village. Hiuen Tsiang, another later visitor from China in the 7th century, also noted the existence of such images of Maitreya.

Throughout the 7th century, Buddhism suffered some decline, as the ruling kings sought to reduce the influence of the faith, if not to eradicate it completely. These kings were Hindus. Famous amongst these rulers was Vikramaditya.

During the 8th century, Tantric ideas crept into the Buddhist traditions and, with these more liberal ideas, the movement against the religion gained strength. Tantric values within Buddhism eventually heralded the decline of the religion across India as Hinduism gained in strength. However, Tantric ideas, which developed in neighbouring Tibet, also grew in influence in Ladakh. Tantra is discussed in a later chapter.

Meanwhile, in Tibet, King Srongtsen Gampo had adopted Buddhism as the state religion of Tibet in the 7th century. It was not until King Trisong Detsen of Tibet invited a series of Indian Buddhist sages and masters to teach Buddhism in Tibet that the religion gained greater favour. Padma Sambhava and later Atisha, Marpa, Naropa and Milarepa all brought new Buddhist ideas to Tibet.

The great revival of Buddhism eluded India, but on the high plateau of Tibet and Ladakh it prevailed. The most far-reaching Buddhist renaissance occurred in Western Tibet and the Guge Kingdom centred on Toling (and Tsaparang). Ironically this revival was in part prompted by the assassination of King Langdarma, a strident Bon practitioner and anti-Buddhist ruler. It was his great-grandson Nyima Gon who really established a firm rule over Ladakh and Western Tibet. Some scholars believe the rock sculptures at Shey were initiated by Nyima Gon.

The eldest son of Nyima Gon ruled Ladakh, while another son held the regions of Ngari to the east in Tibet. The third son was given lower Zanskar, Lahaul and Spiti. The descendants of the second son, Yeshe O and Changchub O, invited the India master Atisha to Toling and thus began the great revival of Buddhism in this region in the 10th–11th centuries. It was at this time that the great translator Rinchen Zangpo helped to establish 108 monasteries across Western Tibet, Spiti and Ladakh.

Rinchen Zangpo is thought to have visited the fledgling monastic centre at Spituk around 1050AD. However, the first of the great Ladakhi monasteries was built in the early 12th century at Likir. During the 12th–15th centuries, the various kings of Ladakh loosely concentrated their power and constructed bridges, palaces and chortens. However, they remained under the influence of Central Tibet.

It was Tsong Khapa, the great Tibetan reformer, who transformed the Kadam-pa sect into the Gelug-pa. Many of the Ladakhi monasteries also transferred allegiance to this sect. Among the monasteries to switch to this yellow-hat sect were Spituk and Likir. Under King Grags Bum-lde, a prolific builder,

Thikse was founded and images of Maitreya constructed at Tingmosgang and Tsemo above Leh. Surprisingly the Sakya-pa monastery at Matho was also consecrated at this time. Links with Tibet continued, with exchange of students and Buddhist teachers.

The lineage of the ruling clique ended with King Lodros Chog Idan, through family dissent. This allowed the Namgyal dynasty to take power. The first king Tashi Namgyal grabbed power from his elder brother but, being unable to produce an heir, rule reverted to the son of his brother, Lhawang. Tashi Namgyal, despite his fairly despotic rule, did bring the Drigung sect, part of the Kagyu-pa discipline from east of Lhasa, into favour.

Tsewang Namgyal (approx 1530–1560) managed by ingenuity to hold power over great swathes of the region; his influence even extended towards Turkish Yarkand. Both Rutok and Guge in Tibet paid tribute to Ladakh. He also built many bridges and attempted to establish a Buddhist college on Tsemo hill at Leh.

Jamyang Namgyal became ruler of Ladakh from 1560–1590. He effectively had to re-subjugate much of his land and then faced a more serious threat from the north and west. The Balti clans had adopted Islam and threatened Ladakh. However, internal bickering for power dented their ability to wage effective war. Conflict took place before the New Year, an inauspicious omen, so the New Year celebration had to be moved forward two months, a date that remains today throughout Ladakh. Jamyang Namgyal retained control, but lost many of his greater lands in the conflict. According to folklore, he had a vision of a lion emerging from a river.

King Sengge (meaning 'lion') Namgyal (approx 1590–1620) became heir to that vision and ruled Ladakh after Jamyang. With the assistance of the Buddhist master Stagsang Raspa (also referred to as Shag Tsang Ras-chen), he founded many new monasteries, including Wanla, Hemis and Chemrey. As a follower of the Druk-pa Kagyu-pa order, he developed Basgo and Hemis further. He also built the nine-storied palace at Leh that remains today. His campaigns to the east allowed him to

19

penetrate into Tibet almost as far as Namring, close to Xigatse. He died on his return at Hanle monastery.

Deldan Namgyal (1620–1640) succeeded his father. One of his brothers, Demchok Namgyal, assumed control over Zanskar and Spiti, ending the rule of the Zanskar kings. Deldan Namgyal was a wise and socially adroit ruler who gave benefits to the people. It was during his rule that the Portuguese Jesuit, Antonio de Andrade, travelled to Tsaparang in Guge, which gave rise to the final decline of the Guge Kingdom.

When the Mongol hordes spread out from Central Asia and effectively took Central Tibet under their wing, if not under full power, the new Ladakhi king Delegs Namgyal found himself on the retreat to Basgo. He turned to Kashmir for help and, under the great Moghul emperor Shah Jahan it was agreed, on condition that he became a Muslim. The first mosques appeared in Leh and have remained to this day, with between 30–50% of the population there being followers of Islam.

From around 1680–1780 a great quarrel for power occurred, beginning with Nyima Namgyal. He ruled wisely and consulted his ministers widely. He also established a printing press for the production of Buddhist texts, as well as the long mani wall in Choglamsar. Another Jesuit missionary, Desideri, passed through Ladakh at the time, around 1715. The king's wife died in childbirth, but another son was born to his second wife. The kingdom was divided between the two heirs, Deskyong and Tashi Namgyal. Family intrigues under Queen Zizi Katan and Puntsog Namgyal reduced the power of Ladakh and it came under threat from Kashmir. In order to resolve the problematic situation of two branches of the family in power over reduced domains, a great lama was dispatched from Tibet as concerns over security surfaced on the plateau.

Rigzin Tsewang Norbu, an emissary of the Dalai Lama, came to Ladakh and, under his guidance, matters were resolved between Purig and central Ladakh. The kings of Zanskar kept power. Tsewang Namgyal, the ruler at the time, was ineffective but no wars took place. His eldest son took power in accordance with the decree of Rigzin Tsewang Norbu.

King Tsestan Namgyal was a wise ruler, played polo well and kept the peace. He built a long mani wall in Leh before his early death. In the absence of an heir, his brother Tsepal took power, having spent his youthful years in Hemis monastery. He ruled until 1841. Despite his indolence, the country prospered, most likely due to the diligence of the chief minister Tsewang Dondrub.

William Moorcroft visited Ladakh around the period 1820–1822, the first British subject to explore the land. Tsepal came under threat from the south when the Kulu kings invaded much of southern Ladakh. The second son of Tsepal, Chogsprul, took three wives in 1834, but his rule was doomed by the rising power of the Sikhs, Ranjit Singh of Lahore, the Dogras of Jammu and the British East India Company.

The Dogras made their way to Ladakh from the south, because the Sikhs held Kashmir at the time. The Ladakhi army was no match for the well-armed and trained forces of Zorawar. However, some resistance was offered and deals struck with the Sikhs to overcome the aggressors. Tsepal Namgyal and Zorawar met at Basgo and a truce was agreed. Little happened in reality; the old King Tsepal was forced to pay tributes and his son Chogsprul left under a cloud for Spiti, never to be heard of again. Milan Singh, the Sikh governor of Kashmir, had pretensions to Ladakh but, despite the intrigues, Tsepal remained in nominal control and the status quo remained.

Not content with his successes in Ladakh, the Dogra chieftain, Zorawar made a brief advance to the north against Muslim Baltistan. To cross the rivers they took to ingenious ice and wood bridges constructed by the Dards of the Indus River on the route to Skardu. The old King Tsepal succumbed on the return journey and his grandson Jigsmed inherited the throne.

Immediately after this assault on the Baltis, Zorawar set his armies, including Ladakhis, towards Tibet. With six to seven thousand men, he crossed the high passes in winter, trashed Hanle and Trashigang monasteries and advanced towards Mount Kailash. At Tirthapuri the Tibetans offered resistance and, soon after, Zorawar was wounded. Rutok, Guge and

Purang were back in the hands of Tibet and Zorawar's grave was built near Purang, where remains still exist today. Peace ensued between Tibet and Ladakh after some years, and Jigsmed Namgyal retired to his palace in Stok.

Some Observations from 1846 and 1847

The men of Ladakh wear a cloak (called la-pa-sha) of woollen, thick and warm. It is usually white, or rather it has once been white; for as the people only wash themselves once a year, and never wash their clothes, their cloaks are always of a dirty hue...

Amongst the upper classes tea is drunk two or three times a day. It is made in a strong decoction with soda, then seasoned with salt and churned with butter, until it acquires the colour and consistency of thick rich cocoa or chocolate...

All classes are extremely fond of spirituous liquors, although they have nothing better than their own indigenous *chang*. This is made from fermented barley and wheat flour, and has a most disagreeable sour smell, like that of bad beer, and a thick appearance like dirty gruel. This is the usual beverage; but it is sometimes distilled, by which process a clear spirit is obtained, something like whiskey, but of a most villainous flavour.

Ladak: Physical, Statistical and Historical
Alexander Cunningham 1853

Under the British, Ladakh remained under Jammu, with monasteries retaining their land and status. The descendants of the Royal Family continued to live at Stok, but all power resided in Srinagar. After partition an uneasy period of Muslim-Buddhist friction continued, but in general Ladakh has been a peaceful place for the last 50 years. In 1947 it formally became part of the Indian state of Jammu and Kashmir.

The Indian army has a strong presence here, partly because of the continuing border disputes with their neighbour Pakistan. Their activities are also concerned with security following border skirmishes with China after the 1962 invasion of a vast part of the country east of the Pangong Lake area. Tibet of course ceased to exercise any sovereign powers after 1959. An exciting road to Manali over the Rohtang Pass, an alternative to the historic route via Kargil, Dras and the Zoji La pass, has been constructed. With political turmoil in Kashmir, Ladakh has eased into a more independent state, with direct air links with Delhi. Tourism has become a major new contributor to the economy.

The Lost Years of Jesus

It is said that Buddhists documented the Life of Saint Issa (Jesus) two thousand years ago, when he travelled in the east and spent some years in India. The Russian explorer and journalist Nicolas Notovitch was travelling in Asia around 1887. When he reached Mulbekh, he heard rumours of manuscripts proving that Jesus had been in Ladakh, and determined to find them. After hearing several more tales hinting at the same, he reached Hemis, where the lama told him secretively that if he came back a second time he may be able to let him see the documents. Finding an excuse to return again and spend more time there, he was able to gain the respect of the lamas, who showed him the documents.

"The name of Issa is held in great respect by the Buddhists," the head lama said. "Our gompa, among others, already possesses a large number (of scrolls brought by students or lamas from Lhasa). Among them are to be found descriptions of the life and acts of the Buddha Issa, who preached the holy doctrine in India and amongst the Israelites and was put to death by pagans... The documents brought from India to Nepal and from Nepal to Tibet concerning his existence are written in the Pali language and are now in Lhasa."

As a result of his research, he wrote The Unknown Life of Jesus Christ: The Life of Saint Issa. This caused great controversy, as many Christians were unable to accept that Jesus had been to India and the East. In particular, an Oxford professor Max Muller poured scorn on the idea and tried to disprove it. His friend Swami Abhedananda visited Hemis in 1922 to check out Nicolas Notovitch's story. Born in 1866, he was an enthusiastic scholar and excellent linguist, particularly keen on Eastern and Western literature. He became a disciple of the Indian saint Ramakrishna, making pilgrimages to holy places across the subcontinent. Then, in 1896, he went to London, now wearing western clothes, and began to preach Hindu philosophy. Here he met Max Muller. After this Swami Abhedananda went to America to preach, but eventually he was able to follow his 'cherished dream' and visit the Himalaya. Visiting Hemis at last, his story more-or-less corroborated the facts given by Notovitch.

At around the same time, the celebrated philosopher, artist and explorer Nicholas Roerich also visited Hemis and quotes some of the same verses in Altai Himalaya, the fascinating travelogue of his journeys through Central Asia and the Tibetan plateau. He writes, *"in every city, in every encampment of Asia, I tried to unveil what memories were cherished in the folk-memory. Through these guarded and preserved tales, you may recognise the reality of the past. In every spark of folklore there is a drop of the great truth adorned or distorted."*

Ten years later, a Swiss woman Elisabeth Caspari, who was a music teacher and member of the Western Zoroastrian movement, and American Mrs Clarence Gasque, head of the World Fellowship of Faith, were at Hemis, A lama presented some papers to them freely, without the two women having any concept of their significance or the historical controversy they had caused.

24

As a result of research using the above sources, it is thought that one possible route Jesus may have taken is as follows:

Departing from Jerusalem, he went north to Damascus, east to Baghdad, across the Iranian desert to Afghanistan and Kabul, across the Khyber Pass and down to Lahore. Going south to Karachi, he then crossed the middle of India to a place called Juggernaut southwest of Calcutta. From here he went up to Kapilvastu and through Kathmandu to Lhasa in Tibet.

On his return journey he is thought to have travelled through Tibet as far west as Mount Kailash, then northwest to Ladakh. From here he went to Srinagar, back to Lahore and Kabul, then through southern Afghanistan and Kandahar to Shiraz in southern Iran then back up to Baghdad, Damascus and Jerusalem.

All these possible routes are discussed by Elizabeth Clare Prophet in her book The Lost Years of Jesus: see Bibliography.

Chapter Three

RELIGION IN LADAKH

Leh is a remarkable site. Here the legends connect the paths of Buddha and Christ. Buddha went through Leh northwards. Issa communed here with the people on his way from Tibet. Secretly and cautiously the legends are guarded. It is difficult to sound them because lamas, above all people, know how to keep silent. Only by means of a common language – and not merely that of tongue but also of inner understanding – can one approach their significant mysteries.
Altai Himalaya: *Nicholas Roerich*

In Leh and its surrounding valleys there are almost too many monasteries to count. As well as the Buddhist temples, there are also several mosques, a Sikh temple and Christian church, and all religions coexist most of the time in perfect harmony.

For the purposes of this book we need concern ourselves mainly with Buddhism.

Buddhism in Ladakh

Although Buddhism is thought of as a religion, it is in many ways more a way of living, a code of practice, a search for peace of mind and an end to suffering.

Prince Gautama Siddhartha, who became the Buddha, was born the son of a king near present-day Lumbini in southern Nepal. His early life was one of luxury; he married the daughter of a neighbouring Raja. In his 29th year he suddenly became aware that there was more to life than he knew, so he left his wife and newborn son to take up the life of an ascetic. He wandered far and wide listening to sages, wise men and Brahmin priests, but could find no solace. After many temptations and much thoughtful meditation he became enlightened, choosing a pathway of acceptance of all suffering. Thus began Buddhism, in approximately 600BC.

Tantra and the form of Buddhism known as Vajrayana later influenced some of the original Buddhist practices. Many adherents in India decried the general liberalisation of pure Buddhism by Tantric ideas. Some believe the Tantric ideas predate both Buddhism and Hinduism, being both ritualistic and pagan in their ancient format. Tibetan Buddhist Tantra developed around the 11th century, with the Kalachakra elements that relate to the Kangyur Tibetan scripts. Kalachakra is the protector who turns the wheel of life.

Tibetan Buddhism incorporated many ideas of the original Bonpo animistic ideas, ideas that had formed the earliest religious practices in Tibet.

Buddhism appears quite different from Hinduism at first sight, but Buddha is considered by Hindus to be an avatar — an incarnation of God. In one of the famous Hindu lyric poems, Vishnu is praised as the great God who, in the guise of Buddha, taught us kindness to all living beings and prohibited animal sacrifices. There are indeed some important doctrinal differences between Hinduism and Buddhism, but Buddha himself lived and died a Hindu and the two religions are closely intertwined.

> *When talking about the nature of impermanence we must bear in mind that there are two levels. One is the coarse level, which is quite obvious and is the cessation of a life or an event. But the impermanent nature which is being taught in the 'Four Noble Truths' refers to the more subtle aspect of impermanence, which is the transitory nature of existence.*
> **Daily Advice from the Heart: *Dalai Lama***

Buddhist Tenets
The philosophy of Buddhism is based on the four noble truths and the eight noble paths, which are as follows:

Four noble truths
These are firstly the truth of **suffering**, which occurs through the cycle of rebirth cycle called *samsara*. The second truth is the **desire** for things, which will always lead to dissatisfaction when they cannot be obtained. **Nirvana**, or the cessation of desire, is the third truth, and the fourth is the way of the **middle path** as a solution.

Eight noble paths
These are the eight ways to attain the path to Nirvana. They are: right understanding, right thought, right speech, right action, right livelihood, right effort, right mind and right concentration.

Dharma means change, *chos* in Tibetan. It is a spiritual transformation.

Principal Tibetan Buddhist Sects

Nyingma-pa

Nyingma-pa is the oldest Tibetan Buddhist sect; its adherents are known as the Red Hat sect. It developed under King Trisong Detsen, who requested the Indian master Santarakshita to teach about Indian Buddhism in Tibet. In 765AD Padma Sambhava, the Indian Tantric sage and magician, was invited to Tibet by at the behest of Santarakshita. The ideas flourished under the Indian Tantrics. Tantra, in essence, uses the powers of mind expansion by any method. It postulates that a person can make his own path to enlightenment without the aid of teachers, collective meditations and reading of scriptures. Tantric practices were later corrupted when the use of sensual pleasure spread into the meditation techniques. Contacts were established between India and Tibet, with many texts being translated. Padma Sambhava, later known as Guru Rinpoche, is generally considered to be the founder of Lamaism in Tibet. His image is often fierce; he frowns and carries a skull-laden staff and a vajra or dorje, the thunderbolt symbol. The Nyingma-pa and the Bon share many features.

Guru Rinpoche's consort Yeshe Tsogyal wrote down many of the teachings of her mentor and these scriptures, known as *termas*, have been concealed to be revealed to future masters, called *tertons,* to propagate the teachings when time dictates they are deemed appropriate. The Dzogchen tantras are revered by the Nyingma-pa and the Bon. These teachings offer quick access to the path of enlightenment. These methods were considered heretical by many followers, as the included methods use sensual and sexual techniques. The Dzogchen tantras include the Tibetan Book of the Dead, known as the Bardo Thodol.

Today the Nyingma-pa sect is still found in Tibet and, in particular, in the Khumbu region of Nepal around Mount Everest.

Kadam-pa

The Kadam-pa was developed in the 11th century after a Bonpo rebellion. It was developed by Atisha, another Indian teacher, a prince, a priest and an intellectual from the great Buddhist university of Nalanda. One of his disciples was Dromton (Drontonpa), who later established a small sect. Atisha held the view that Tantric methods to enlightenment should only follow on from prior in-depth reflection on the philosophy of the religion. Some believe that the austere practices of the sect led to it being eclipsed by the powerful Sakya-pa sect. The Kadam-pa later became the basis of the Yellow Hat sect, the dominant Gelug-pas.

Kagyu-pa

The Kagyu-pa is a sect is attributed to the Indian mystic translator (Lotsawa) Marpa, a disciple of Atisha. He followed in the path of the other famous India sages, Tilopa and Naropa, who are also considered masters of Kagyu-pa. Marpa lived from 1012–1097 and it was he who translated what are known as the Guhyasamaja and Cakrasamvara Tantras. Marpa's student Milarepa became the Kagyu-pa's most famous great saint, as well as being a hermit and poet. In his early life he practised black magic. After he reformed he lived in isolation in the Himalaya. One of his more famous cave dwellings is near

Nyalam, just across the border from Nepal, in Tibet. The Kagyu-pa sect look inwards to concentrate their meditations on inner mental and spiritual matters, and above all to be close to their teachers. Many of the Kagyu-pa texts have been derived from firstly the Vajradhara texts and later from the Guhyasamaja Tantra, Cakrasamvara Tantra and the Hevajra texts.

The Kagyu-pa sect has adopted a number of sub-groups, such as the Dagpo, Drigung-pa, Druk-pa, Taglung-pa and the Karma-pa from Tsurphu, whose disputed reincarnates have become well known in recent years.

Karma-pa (Karmarpa)

The Karma-pa (Karmarpa) is one of the more well-known of the main sub-sects of the Kagyu-pa. It descended from the master, Gampopa (1079–1153), whose life was reputedly foretold by Buddha Sakyamuni. His student Dusum Khyenpa (1110–1193) became the first teacher of the Drigung sect, building the monasteries at Tsurphu and in the province of Kham. There have been a total of sixteen re-incarnates. The 17th incarnate Lama was recognised in Tibet in 1992. The Black Hat Karmarpas are just one influential body within the sect; they are famous for their festival dances.

The **Taglung-pa**, which followed more austere disciplines, has largely been obscured by the Gelug-pa doctrines that followed. The sub-sect called Phagmodru Kagyu-pa of the Dagpo Kagyu-pa has its head monastery at Dentsathil.

Drigung-pa

The Drigung sect has its founding monastery of Drigung Til about 125km northeast of Lhasa above the Kyi Chu river. Its founder was a Kham monk who was known as Jigten Sumgon. He lived from 1143–1217. In Ladakh he is called Skyoba Jigten.

Druk-pa

The Druk-pa have two main regions of influence. The northern Druk-pa are found in Tibet and Ladakh. The southern Druk-pa are found in Bhutan. The sect was formed in the 12th century in Ralung, near Gyangtse in southern Tibet. Because of persecution by Gelug-pa followers, many Druk-pa lamas left for Bhutan around this time. The Shabdrung, the spiritual leader of the Druk-pa sect, was a descendant of the original founder of Ralung monastery, and in 1616 he also left Tibet for Bhutan, where the Druk-pa lineage developed and flourished in a unique way.

Sakya-pa

The Sakya-pa started in the 11th century south of modern-day Lhatse, not far west of Xigatse. Konchok Gyalpo, who founded Sakya monastery, was a pupil of Drogmi, who had also studied at Nalanda. This sect stresses the need for study of existing Buddhist scriptures. Learning and study are its main themes, with less of the Tantric or physical elements. By 1220 the Sakya-pa predominated in Tibet. Its greatest proponent was Kunga Gyetsan, a Buddhist adherent who laid the foundations for cooperation between Tibet and Mongolia around 1247. Under the Sakya-pa, the two great Tibetan Buddhist bibles, the Tangyur and Kangyur, were compiled. The Sakya-pa declined when Tsong Khapa, the next reformer, appeared.

Gelug-pa

The Gelug-pa is the Yellow Hat sect of the Dalai Lama. Tsong Khapa was the initiator and reformer of this sect. He reformed the earlier ideas of Atisha from the 14th century. This form of Buddhism reverted to a more purist format, bringing a higher degree of morality and discipline to the monk body. It sought to exorcise some of the Tantric aspects and to cleanse the religion. The first monastery was established at Ganden near Lhasa. The large monasteries of Drepung and Sera in Lhasa and Tashi Lhunpo in Xigatse belong to this sect. The Gelug-pa sect is now the dominant group in Tibet and they still follow the lineage of the Dalai Lamas as their spiritual leader.

Significant Tibetan Buddhist Deities

Adi Buddha The Buddha without beginning or end, the infinite self-created Buddha; the primordial Buddha. Vajradhara is the name of the Adi Buddha when he is represented either in single form or in yab-yum with his consort. Occasionally the Adi Buddha can be seen nude; in this form he is called Samantabhadra and is also recognised as such by the Tibetan Nyingma-pa sect.

Sakyamuni (Sakya Tukpa) The pure image of the mortal Buddha, Gautama Siddhartha, born in Nepal. He often has blue hair, a golden body and holds a bowl in his lap in most depictions.

The **Dhyani Buddhas** face the four cardinal directions, meditating, and are abstract images encompassing the universe. Gyawa Ri Gna is their Tibetan name. These five mystical Buddhas are found in the Mahayana form of Buddhism that developed over the subcontinent. The Dhyani Buddhas were created from the meditation and wisdom of the Adi Buddha, the primordial Buddha. The Dhyani Buddhas in turn evolved into the Dhyani Bodhisattvas, who gave creation to the universe. Some of these then gave us the human or mortal teachers.

Vairocana The first Dhyani Buddha and resides in the stupa sanctum. He is the cosmic element, who cannot be shown. On occasion he appears on the east side of large stupas (e.g. Swayambhu in Kathmandu). Vairocana is the illuminator who lights the way.

Akshobhya The Dhyani Buddha who sits facing east. He is regarded as the second Dhyani; he looks similar to Ratna Sambhava, but his right hand has its palm facing inwards. Akshobhya has various wrathful forms, including Heruka.

Amitabha The oldest of the Dhyani Buddhas, he always faces west. The Amitabha Buddha is linked to Sakyamuni, the earthly Buddha. Opagme is his Tibetan name. **Aparmita** is a version of Amitabha with his hands clasping a vase on his lap.

The Panchen Lama is considered to be his earthly representative.

Amoghasiddhi The Dhyani Buddha who always faces north. When on a stupa or chorten, a serpent with seven heads usually stands behind him. This Dhyani Buddha is linked to the future Buddha, Maitreya.

Ratna Sambhava The Dhyani Buddha who faces south; his right hand has its palm facing outwards. He is yellow in colour.

Vajrasattva The sixth Dhyani Buddha. He is the priest for the other five, and is only found separately from his disciples. He carries a vajra and a bell. Vajrasattva is considered to be the Adi Buddha by the Kadam-pa Tibetan sect.

Amitayus The Buddha of Boundless Life; an aspect of Amitabha; the Buddha associated with longevity practice and empowerment of longevity. He is found seated with a vase in his hands. In Tibet he is referred to as Tsepame. Those meditating on Amitayus are performing meditation on Kriya Tantra, meaning limitless life.

Bodhisattva A saint or disciple of Buddha, who has delayed the attainment of Nirvana and has remained to teach. They are found in the Mahayana path of Buddhism. The term can be confusing. Translated literally, it comes from *bodhi*, meaning highest consciousness, and *sattva*, meaning reality or essence within the living.

Avalokiteshvara (Chenresig) A popular and famous bodhisattva. He has renounced Nirvana, the end of the cycle of rebirth. He embodies compassion (Karuna) and remains on earth to counter distress and suffering. He is believed by many to be the creator of our universe. Avalokiteshvara in one aspect is quite commonly seen in visual form with eleven heads and eyes on his hands. The **Dalai Lama** is considered to be his earthly representative.

This strange symbolism was explained to me by a lama, who was almost carried away by his own eloquence: "Chenresig is filled with infinite compassion for all creatures. You simply cannot imagine how compassionate he is. As he saw their constant sufferings and struggles in the Round of Existence, from which they vainly sought a way of escape, so overcome with pity was he that his head burst and was shivered into fragments. Then his own lama, the Buddha of Infinite Light (the same who emanates into the Panchen Lama of Tashi Lhunpo), provided him with a fresh head and this happened no less than ten times.

Peaks and Lamas: *Marco Pallis*

Lokeshvara Lord of the world, with 108 different versions (bodhisattvas). Avalokiteshvara is the most commonly found version, being the one who came back to earth to save mankind. Lokeshvara appears in some forms with two or many heads.

Padmapani Another version of Lokeshvara linked to the Dhyani Buddha, Amitabha. He is seen with the lotus displayed prominently. He is generally white, but is also red in one version.

Vajrapani (Channa Dorje) Spiritual son of Dhyani Buddha Akshobhya. He carries a dorje (vajra) and is a powerful wrathful protector in Tibet. He has monstrous Tantric powers and wears a snake around his neck. In this aspect he is related to the nagas, with whom he is associated in Nepal. Vajrapani is the conveyor of the Tantric texts and a bodhisattva of energy. Vajrapani is also a spiritual son of Dhyani Buddha Akshobhya. He is linked to Garuda in legend and in aspect. He carries a vajra.

Hayagriva (Tamdrin) Wrathful emanation of Chenresig who guards many shrines. He is seen in blood red with a small horse sticking out of his head. He wears a garland of skulls and has bird-like wings on his back. Tamdrin has a link to Vishnu and has wings on his back like Garuda.

Manjushri (Jampelyang) God of divine wisdom. He carries the sword which cuts through ignorance. According to tradition he is a Chinese saint. To worship Manjushri gives intellect and intelligence. Manjushri is a popular bodhisattva and is considered to be the first divine teacher of Buddhism, giving inspiration.

Yamantaka (Dorje Jigje) 'Slayer of death', a wrathful emanation of Manjushri. He is the one who can destroy Yama, the guardian at the gates of heaven and hell. Yama is the deity who holds the wheel of life in his jaws. He is also known as **Vajrabhairab** and has a buffalo head. These wrathful deities are not actual demons but represent the idea of demons in the mind to be exorcised and replaced by compassion.

Chakra Sambhava (Demchok) Guardian deity of Mount Kailash. He is normally seen in blue and holds the dorje. He is said to represent the union of bliss and emptiness when seen in yab-yum with his consort Dorje Phagmo (Vajra Varahi). Demchok is a Tantric meditation deity. Demchok also appears as Heruka, a meditation deity. Chakra (Cakra) means wheel.

Drolma (Dolma) The Sanskrit **Tara** who is sacred to both Buddhists and Hindus. She represents the maternal aspect, symbolising fertility, purity and compassion. Tara can appear in different colours, red, green, white, gold, and as Kali, dark blue. Each represents a different aspect of her nature. There are considered to be twenty-one aspects or forms of Drolma. Tara helps one to rise from previous sin into a new beginning. Tara is often depicted with eyes in her hands and feet.

Drolkar (White Tara) Born of a tear from the bodhisattva, Avalokiteshvara, a compassionate saviour and disciple of Buddha past. She is a consort of Vairocana, the first Dhyani Buddha. She is worshipped for long life, and for healing. She has seven eyes, three in her head, with two in each of her hands and feet.

Green Tara Most often associated with the Nepalese **Princess Bhrikuti** who married the Tibetan king Srongtsen Gampo. She is worshipped for liberation from danger. She is also linked spiritually to Amoghasiddhi, the Dhyani Buddha, and inspires good in women.

Tara also has a ferocious form called **Ekajata**. She is seen standing on a corpse, has a third eye, is dwarf-like, ugly and usually blue. Ugratara also means a terrible version of Tara and is linked to the Vajra Yogini, who is rarely seen in Ladakh. The rare **Red Tara** is called Kurukulla. There are twenty-one different aspects of Tara.

Palden Lhamo Another female deity sometimes linked to the blue Kali of the Hindus. She is a protectress of the Gelug-pa. A backdrop of peacock feathers sits behind her and she holds a corpse in her mouth.

Dipankar An unusual deity. He is the enlightener, and is normally red in colour. At his birth, bright lights appeared miraculously. He is said to be a Buddha of a previous cosmic or life cycle and is rarely seen in Ladakh.

Maitreya Buddha (Chamba or Jampa) The future Buddha to come; appears in a number of monasteries. His colour is yellow or gold and he is said to be preparing to come to earth. He usually stands, or sits with his legs pointing downwards. Maitreya is found in abundance in Ladakh.

Medicine Buddha (Menlha) Engaged for healing the sick. He is often a blue colour and seen with four hands. In some chapels one may see eight versions of this Buddha. The Medicine Buddhas feature in quite a number of monastery paintings.

Prajnaparamita Probably the most popular deity within Vajrayana. She is the goddess of superior wisdom and can shine a light on the way to Nirvana. Prajnaparamita (and Vajratara) both confer wisdom and emanate from the five Dhyani Buddhas. The Prajnaparamita tantras are a major source of wisdom in Tibetan Buddhism.

Vijaye A goddess, a bodhisattva, one of the three deities of longevity. Her Tibetan name is Namgyalma. She has three heads and six arms, and embodies victory and fearlessness.

Mahakala (Nagpo Chenpo) One of the eight aspects of terror; he can be exceedingly ugly and ferocious in art forms. He is rather like the terrible Hindu god Bhairab and often tramples on bodies or corpses. He has strong links to Shiva through Bhairab and his trident. Mahakala is a vision of the wrathful Avalokiteshvara and is used for training the mind.

Mahakala is also known as **Gonpo** in Ladakh, the great black one. Dharmapala is another name sometimes given to an aspect of Mahakala. But what are his adornments for, the ones that make us quiver? Mahakala is always black or dark blue; he has three eyes, which represent the past, present and future. His ghostly crown of skulls or gruesome heads represents the five delusions that poison a soul. These are ignorance, anger, desire, jealousy and pride. His sword is there to cut through ego, while the skull-cup of blood is to show his powers over wrongdoing. The necklace of skulls denotes his efforts to aid all beings, and when he stamps on animals it means he is crushing all obstacles to enlightenment. Wearing a tiger skin and other animal items, he suppresses anger and attains purification from the primary poisons of the soul.

Mahakali The great blackness, an extreme form of Kali.

Kubera Lord of wealth and guardian of the treasures of the world. Buddhists worship Kubera as **Jambhala**. He sits on a dragon sideways, and is attended by a mongoose that vomits jewels.

Vajra Varahi A red goddess who embodies the five wisdoms and pleasures. She appears nude and is sometimes seen trampling on Bhairab. She was a consort of Padma Sambhava / Guru Rinpoche.

Vajradhara One of the highest deities. He appears either single or in the Buddhist Yab-Yum male-female embrace. Vajradhara is considered by the Tibetan Kagyu-pa sect to be the primordial or Adi Buddha.

Kalachakra A yoga Tantric deity. He can be seen with four faces, normally twenty-four arms, and usually stands on two figures on a lotus plinth. He is the deity of the wheel of time. His tiny yab-yum consort is Vishvamati.

37

Guhyasamaja A meditation deity as well as a Tantric scripture, associated primarily with the Nyingma-pa teachings.

Padma Sambhava / Guru Rinpoche The lotus-born Tantric master who established Vajrayana Buddhism in Tibet in the 8th–9th century at the invitation of King Trisong Detsen. The Nyingma-pa Red Hat sect began at around the same time. In Tibet he tamed hostile spirits and made it possible to build Samye monastery. Although he was able to learn the teachings spontaneously, he pretended to have to study in order to instil confidence in ordinary people. He hid various important teachings in Tibet, Nepal and Bhutan, in order that they may be revealed for future generations in years to come. He was also known as **Padma Kara**. One of his consorts was **Yeshe Tsogyal**, another was Mandavara. For further details, see the box about Padma Sambhava at the end of this section.

Tsong Khapa Known in Tibet as Jerinpoche, he is the founder of the Gelug-pa sect. He usually wears a yellow pointed hat. He often sits between two similar Buddha figures called Gyeltsab Je and Khedrub Je.

The **fifth Dalai Lama**, Lobsang Gyatso, can be confused in paintings with Tsong Khapa, but he holds a dharma wheel and lotus flower.

Milarepa Tibet's poet saint, was an historical figure, around whom many legends have grown up. In his 'Hundred Thousand Songs' he left Tibet perhaps its greatest poetic legacy. Living as a human being, he suffered all the highs and lows of human existence before achieving realisation. After being first a disciple of Buddha, he later became a Buddha himself.

Dakini means 'born of the pure realm.' A dakini is a female deity, a demon goddess who can fly; she represents the emptiness that is found in the nature of reality. She is the female partner in Tantric union, a female Tantric deity who protects and serves the Buddhist doctrine and practitioners. Vajra Varahi and Vajra Yogini are often classified as dakinis. The male counterpart of a dakini is a **Daka**: a male practitioner of Vajrayana.

Khandro A dakini or one who travels through space, a space voyager.

The Four Harmonious Brothers
In many Tibetan and Buddhist monasteries are paintings depicting four animals, one on top of the other. These are the Elephant, the Monkey, the Rabbit and the Bird on top. These represent the harmony that can act as a direction for peace and removal of conflict.

The Four Guardians known as the **Lokapalas** are the deities seen at the entrance to most monasteries. **Dhitarashtra** is the guardian of the east; he is white and holds a flute. **Virupaksha** guards the west; he is red with a stupa in his right hand and a serpent in his left hand. **Virudhakla** is guardian of the south and holds a blue sword. **Vaishravana** is guardian of the north; he has a yellow banner in his right hand and a mongoose in his left hand, which usually is seen vomiting jewels. He is also called Jambhala.

Mahasiddha A Tantric yogin or yogini (meditator) with siddhi, the spiritual accomplishment. Maha means great. There are said to be eighty-four Mahasiddhas of ancient India in Tantric literature.

The Early Life of Padma Sambhava (Guru Rinpoche)

Padma Sambhava was an 8th century India Buddhist sage and Tantric magician, who was invited to Tibet by Santarakshita, an India Buddhist master. With his great spiritual power, he created the conditions for the propagation of the teachings of Vajrayana Buddhism in this world in the 8th century. He hid various important teachings, in order that they could be revealed to future generations.

In Sanskrit Padma means lotus flower, and Sambhava means born from. In Tibet and Ladakh, Padma Sambhava is also known as Guru Rinpoche.

According to legends there was a king, Indrabodhi, who had no son. He was a kind ruler, but one day he ran out of money. He knew that on an island lived the naga king's daughter, who possessed a great jewel that would satisfy all wishes. After crossing oceans and fending off demons, the king finally reached the golden island and retrieved the precious jewel. On his way home, he saw an eight-year-old boy sitting alone on another island, carrying a vajra in one hand and a lotus in the other.

The king spoke to him, and, realising from that he must be a wise emanation, took him for his son. When he returned home he asked the jewel to restock his treasury, which was miraculously done. Then the king gave alms to all who asked: clothes for the cold, food for the hungry, and a shower of gems for the poor. He told them all they must study and practise Mahayana Buddhism.

The son and prince was Padma Sambhava, and as the prince grew up, he realised that he could not benefit the people by ruling the kingdom. So he murdered the son of one of the ministers, in order that he would be banished. He was sent to live in the charnel grounds among the corpses. One day he heard about an evil king named Shakraraja. Padma went to his land wearing the skin of the corpses as his clothing. He ate the flesh of the males and copulated with the females. He brought everyone under his power and was known as the Rakshasa demon; he became a powerful yogi.

Then, having pondered on the troubles of the world, he approached two monks and said, "I will not do any more evil; please accept me," as he handed over his weapons. They sent him to their master, who taught him more Yoga Tantra. In order to practise the 'secret mantra', Padma Sambhava found a beautiful young maiden. They went together to the Cave of Maratika, and after three months they saw a vision of Amitayus.

He blessed them both, master Padma as Hayagriva (a protector) and his consort as Vajra Varahi (a boar-headed female deity).

When Padma and his consort returned to his homeland, the people recognised him as the man who had killed the son of their minister, and tried to burn them both to death. However, the fire was still burning after twenty-one days, and all were afraid to go and look. But the king, who was Padma Sambhava's father, thought, "If he really is a miraculous emanation, then he won't burn." So he went to have a look. Sitting in the middle of a huge lake were Padma and his consort, adorned with garlands of skulls in order to liberate beings through compassion. The king was filled with wonder.

Later, from a historical point of view, Padma was invited to Tibet by King Trisong Detsen around 747AD. He is generally credited as being the founder of Tibetan Lamaism, mixing Mahayana Buddhism and the existing Bonpo cults together. Padma was a teacher of the Tantric school. In Tibet he is revered by the Red Hat or old school, Nyingma-pa sect, and is known as Guru Rinpoche.

As Guru Rinpoche he travelled across Tibet meditating in many caves along the way, including one below Mount Kailash. His main task in Tibet, according to legends, was to subjugate the local spirits. These Bon spirits constantly sought to destroy his attempts to build the holy temple of Samye monastery. But on his journey he manifested as a fierce character, terrifying all who saw him. In this way Samye monastery was finally built. After creating Samye monastery, he intended to return to India, but in fact he did not do so for approximately 56 years, so it is said...

Tantra in Ladakh

In Sanskrit, Tantra means liberation, an expansion of ideas. Taken literally, it means an expansion tool, a way of increasing the awareness of the mind to reach the divine level.

Some scholars believe that Tantric ideas can be traced to Stone Age art, which evolved from ritualistic pagan ideas. Its origins probably predate all the ancient religious concepts of India, as well as Hinduism and Buddhism. It was transmitted orally until around the 3rd century AD. Its earliest forms were integrated into witchcraft, shamanism, blood sacrifices and other pagan practices. Some of these pagan ideas have survived to manifest today in temple art, festivals and daily rituals.

Later, pagan Tantra was suffocated by new ideas. These new ideas, Hinduism and Buddhism, suggested that all life was a cycle of suffering and rebirth on a path to enlightenment. Tantric themes did influence Buddhism through the Vajrayana path and were still practised quite openly. Its liberal ideas suggested in effect, that 'paradise' was achievable 'now' and that each being could find his own path. Tantra in these forms was virtually obliterated in India by the Muslim invasions of the 12th and 13th centuries. The invaders found the idol worship and liberal concepts totally abhorrent. Hidden behind the Himalaya, though, Tantra survived in Tibet, Ladakh, Nepal and the remoter parts of Assam. See below.

Most forms of Tantra were subject to animistic ideas, with a corrupting of more idealistic thought. However, Tantra also developed in less pagan ways, having both physical and mental strands to reach a complete state of peace. Some people perform Tantric meditation, which does not involve any physical methods, but is purely visual and uses the imagination.

Everything in the physical world is seen as opposites of polarity. Duality is Tantra's prime direction. Within the male-female domain there is some overlap, but each is incomplete without the other. There is suffering. Tantra interweaves the two to make one. There are elements of the female within the male and vice-versa. Balance can only be achieved through the actions of both acting as one. In Tantra the coupling enables the fiery energies to join and the intellects to exchange in order to escape to a higher consciousness.

Tantra seeks to utilise the inner female power to save the world from destruction. One must strive to balance the male-female energy on earth to open up to the cosmos. Tantrics strongly worship the female, both as the true female and the feminine part of the male.

Much of Tantra reaches to the esoteric, far beyond the confines of religion.

Tibetan Tantra

In Tibet, the Tantric ideas originally came from India, together with Buddhism, before the Muslim invasions south of the Himalaya. Tibetan Tantra developed more in the 11th century, as we have discussed earlier. It survived and followed a different path, becoming mixed with the Tibetans' own Bonpo pagan concepts of black magic, sorcery and witchcraft. Tibetan Tantra involves the occult, the magical. Even in modern times these traditional rituals exist. The Oracles, a sort of witch doctor advisor to the high Lamas, were formerly part of the Tibetan state. Some still remain in Ladakh. They use the medium of dance and trance to delve deep into the occult for answers, and to define auspicious moments for celebrating, appeasement and to invoke higher powers.

In its most visual forms, we see Tantric images depicted in the ritual embrace of the deities and the dakinis. Tantric temples often show these deities as ferocious, gruesome demons. In a dark, mysterious chamber of the Potala Palace in Lhasa, there are tall, grotesque, monstrous demons looming and lurking, sending a spine-chilling wave through the imagination. The power of destruction is enough to make one run in terror.

Some Tantrics and Siddhis, those with miraculous powers, are said to be able to project their own consciousness into other beings. We are in the realms of the exoteric now. Within the astral universe, the cosmos filled with good and evil thoughts, playing with fire of this magnitude is indeed playing with the supernatural. Some Tibetans claim to have been able to leave their earthly bodies, experience these supernatural phenomena and return to their living bodies. Such people are known as a *Delog*. Then there are the she-devils, the *lhamos* and the *bhutas*, evil spirits, the dragons of Tibet and Bhutan.

Reincarnation is central to Tibetan Buddhism and here again we find a link to Tantra. Some Tantrics believe that the soul enters a human being or a human condition to achieve its divine purpose. This soul cannot be destroyed, but merely passes from one life to the next. One may never glimpse into past lives, but perhaps in fleeting moments, through premonitions for example, these lives can manifest. Why then do we not reap the benefits of these earlier lives? We do benefit, but for greater understanding we need to be free of past ideas. Some Tantric meditation endeavours to find the truths of earlier existences.

Recently there has been an upsurge of interest in the more physical forms of Tantra. Tantric yoga and Tantric sex are used to shortcut these other methods of finding the desired state of enlightenment, the release from earthly sufferings. The embrace of the couple is both physical and spiritual. Its adherents believe it allows the combined energies to flow, to enable the souls to be taken on to a higher astral plane.

Chapter Four

MONASTERY ART

Buddhist art represents serenity, ferocity, eroticism and ecstasy, seen with equal frequency throughout its different forms. The first visual impression is one of sensory overload. Yet there is some order in the singularly disordered. Buddha images can be numbered in the thousands.

There are many forms of art throughout Ladakh, which can be categorised into three main groupings: statues, with subgroups of clay and metal; paintings, with subgroups of murals and fabrics, such as thangkas; and wood carvings.

All the temples display art forms that relate to the deities and gods. We see in the paintings and statues of Tibetan Buddhism the yab-yum art forms, where gods and demons are in the embrace of female partners. The *yidams*, who are the tutelary divinities, are invariably shown in yab-yum positions. The fierce protectors are often seen clinging on to their partners with especially intense emotion, and with all their limbs, as the fires burn around them. This emphasises the connection between all religious ideas and the cycles of life in creation, birth and death. In the more serene depictions, the lotus flower is often seen as a plinth or base for the gods and deities. The lotus plant is a link for Buddhists to the world of erotic art. It represents the lingam. It is at the heart of the creation of life. Brahma, the creator, was born of a lotus flower. The lotus is pure and from it life will spring.

Above some of the main Buddhas or bodhisattvas one might find some protectors such as the fish-like, demonic-looking figures known as Makaras. A birdman, Garuda or Khyung figure usually sits above all the other images.

Types of Monastery

There are four main designs of Tibetan and Ladakhi monasteries. These are first the mandala style, the design followed by the first monastery in Tibet at Samye. The Toling Yeshe O temple in Guge also exhibits this style. The second design of monastery is found in Ladakh. The Alchi Chos complex is bounded by walls and sits on the plains. A similar style is used at Tabo in Spiti. A third style is found in Bhutan, where courtyards are enclosed by chapels and buildings. Lastly there are the most common formats found in Ladakh, such as Chemrey, Thikse, Phyang, Stakna, Likir and Spituk, which cling to the tops and sides of defensive hillocks and isolated promontories.

Statues

Throughout Ladakh are some amazing examples of bronze and gilded work. Some of the images have been constructed under the guidance of Newari artisans from Nepal. The centres for this art form in Nepal were Patan and also Bhojpur in east Nepal. (See also Chiling in Zanskar later in this book.) Metal sculptures are made by the Lost Wax method. Using this method, wax is used to outline the image, then it is covered with clay. After heating, the wax is drained, and molten metal is poured in. See Bibliography for more information.

Statues, whether made of bronze and gilded metal, or of clay, are invariably elaborate designed and executed by craftsmen. The sculptures are unbelievably intricate, with multiple heads and arms intertwined, teeth and fingernails sharply defined. Most of them are painted in incredibly vivid colours.

Paintings

The same applies to the paintings. Whether frescoes on the monastery walls, or paintings on fabric, such as the beautiful often gold-painted thangkas, exquisite workmanship has survived sometimes hundreds of years, defying the ravages of nature as well as the Cultural Revolution. Some of the paintings need to be studied with a magnifying glass to see the finest detail.

The influence of Kashmiri art, as found in the Guge Kingdom (see History), is seen in the presence of smaller depictions, sometimes of ordinary people in village scenes as opposed to deities. But it is also seen, for example in Alchi, where large paintings of deities or mandalas are surrounded by a huge number of smaller Buddha figures.

Thangkas (tangkas) are Buddhist paintings, which are found in all monasteries in Ladakh. They are sacred scrolls that function as focal points for the practitioner. Traditional thangkas are painted using natural pigments; gold is particularly important. Many depict the stories of the life of Buddha. Most tend to depict a central deity surrounded by lesser figures. Most are from Tibetan Buddhism. Another less common art form is the Tshog-shing (a Tibetan word). In these pictures the central figure is either Gautama Buddha or the long-nosed, yellow-hatted reformer Tsong Khapa. This figure will most often be surrounded by hordes of disciples, witches, divinities, guardians and yidams.

Thangkas were also produced for ordinary people at the behest of their religious teachers. These would often depict the sentiments closest to their hearts, such as desires for long life and happiness. The deities would reflect these desires.

Today thangka painting has developed from being a purely religious skill to become an art form in its own right. Thangkas are now produced for sale to tourists, but retain traditional styles and methods of production. The same artistic skills are used to paint the monastery walls.

Wheel of Life is a graphic representation of life, showing all its mundane aspects. It is a pictorial way of showing us the cycles of life, birth and death into which we are locked by our human desires. These art forms are often found near monastery entrances and follow a general format, with variations depending on the artist.

At the centre are three rather strange animal figures. These are the snake, pig and large bird, which are biting each other. They represent hatred, ignorance and greed. The six main segments depict the realms of different rebirth. The heavenly realm is at the top, and the hellish realm at the bottom. All beings must pass through these different realms. A Buddha figure offers his teachings in each segment. Around the outside are twelve further segments, illustrating the periods of life from birth to death.

The wheel is held by the god Yama – the lord of death – the god who sits in judgement. He is seen tearing and biting it. Buddha is to the right of Yama. He points to a bodhisattva on the left, who can suggest a way out of the wheel, out of suffering, to Nirvana.

Mandalas are other diagrammatic art forms. The geometric shapes within the whole represent the different constituents that help to bring a realisation of enlightenment. Part is the cosmic aspect and other parts are the essence that makes the whole. Circles are the main feature, representing the infinite. Squares represent the form of the universe.

Wood Carving

This art form is not so common in Ladakh, though it is a speciality of neighbouring Kashmir. Generally speaking, woodcarvings are found on doors, frames and on background art, rather than representing the deities themselves. One interesting wooden decorative style is found on the entrance to the Sum Tsek Lhakhang at Alchi. This is called a 'Trifoliate' arch.

Turquoise in Ladakh

The Ladakhi women are often weighed down by their magnificent turquoise headdresses, known as *perak*. These beautiful works of art are an indication of their wealth and status. Young women may start with several beads of glass and mother-of-pearl, but as they get older and acquire more money, they will gradually replace these with turquoise. They may have up to seven rows of between one hundred to four hundred stones, weighing up to three kilos. Placed on top of her head, the *perak* will extend down the woman's back, sometimes well towards her waist. When laid flat, the headdress is shaped like a snake.

The snake is venerated by many Hindu cults in India, and is also an important icon in Vajrayana Buddhism. The best stones are placed at the top of the *perak*, hence the belief that snakes have jewels inside their heads. Snakes, known as *nagas*, are the guardians of the world's mineral wealth, hence the special importance of the shape of the *perak*.

Turquoise is considered the preferred gem for good health and prosperity. A turquoise stone is believed to guard its wearer against evil spirits, demons and the evil eye. More specifically, it is said to have medicinal properties.

Some of the best turquoise found here originates from far western Tibet, in particular from the region of Ngari near the holy Mount Kailash. Some of this valuable turquoise was paid to the kings of Ladakh as tribute by the kings of Guge.

The women of Ladakh still wear turquoise headdresses today, but they tend to be reserved for special occasions and festivals.

Chapter Five

PEOPLE OF LADAKH

The Ladakhi people are mainly Buddhists of Tibetan origin, and their festivals and day-to-day lives reflect this. The climate is much the same as the Tibetan plateau, so the local customs have the same practical values and applications. There is also a significant number of Muslims, because of the proximity to Muslim Kashmir. Many Muslims have lived in Ladakh for generations and are just as much Ladakhi as their Buddhist compatriots.

Women here, however, whether Buddhist or Muslim, are seen working in the streets and may mix with men who are not their close relatives or family. In fact, often the women do the work while the men sit around in tea shops drinking tea!

Traditionally, the women wear uniquely-shaped black top hats, though nowadays these seem to be reserved for older women and special occasions. Both sexes wear thick robes in the ice-cold winter, traditionally sheepskin but now all sorts of man-made fibres and Western clothing too.

Jolly hockey sticks

Everything was white as we drove out of Leh on a frosty morning. All, that is, except the sky, a vivid blue, the sun offering a glimmer of hope of some warmth during the hours of daylight. Ahead of us lay a snow-covered road; alongside were frozen fields, frozen rivers and frozen people. All, that is, except the Indian Army, who were preparing for battle. They marched sternly down the road, hockey sticks at the ready, like rifles. The ice rink was a frozen field at the roadside. At least this battle would have a friendly outcome.

Normally there are no inter-ethnic problems between Buddhists and Muslims, though being near to the Indian/Pakistani Line of Control can occasionally cause the situation to flare up temporarily.

Customs: Birth, Marriage and Death

Below are the traditional rituals and ceremonies carried out at important moments in life. Nowadays these are not so strictly followed by everyone.

Birth: Tsa Ton

Tsa Ton is the celebration that takes place after a child is born. The party takes place at the mother's house. All relatives bring gifts according to their means; cloth, food or money. They depart with a bowl of *chang*, the local home-brewed beer. Traditionally, the mother remains at home with her new baby for a month and ten days, though this is not strictly followed nowadays. One year later, the child is named. This feast is called **Ming Ton**. Mother and child present a great lama with food and grain from the family, and the lama names the child. Then a big party with lots of drinking and dancing takes place at their home.

Marriage: Bag Ton

This is traditionally a very formal feast. After the engagement, the groom goes to his fiancée's house with a large quantity of *chang* to discuss the date of the marriage and other formalities. From this time on he must send good food and chang every day to his beloved. Twenty days later, both sides of the family get together to witness the groom giving a present to his prospective mother-in-law. This may be money, ornaments, jewellery or simply chang. Two weeks later, both sides of the family meet again at the bride's house and take her in state to the groom's house, where a group of lamas is waiting. Prayers are read, then the happy couple are pronounced man and wife. A great feast now follows, with abundant chang and delicious food for all. This may continue for more than a week. Every day begins with lama's prayers for those who are not too drunk to listen.

Death: Shid Ton

There are various traditional methods of disposing of a dead body and ensuring a good passage of the soul to its next reincarnation, depending on the wealth of the deceased. If the family is rich, a large number of lamas are sent for. They will read prayers every day until the body is cremated. This continues for fifteen days and nights. For poorer families there may be only one lama and he may come for only five days. While mourning, a piece of cloth covers the door to the house. During this period the lama(s) are fed by the family. On the day of cremation, the clothes and cooking utensils of the deceased are given to the lamas. The ashes, known as the *Purthal*, are collected and mixed with clay to make an image of the dead person. A chorten is built to house the remains and various articles must be placed there also: wheat, barley, rice and peas; pearls, coral and turquoise; gold, silver and copper, plus iron; prayers and holy writings; sandalwood. Nowadays not all families can afford these, but something similar must traditionally be offered.

Because Ladakh is critically short of wood to burn, the dead are often bound into a sitting position so they can be burnt on a smaller surface area and thus use less wood. Or they may be chopped into small pieces by professional 'body choppers' and then fed to the dogs. This sort of funeral is also preceded by lamas' prayers for the deceased. This is known as an **Earth Funeral**.

Another method is the **Celestial Funeral**, or **Sky Burial**, in which case the bones are completely cleaned of flesh and are then pounded into a paste, mixed with corn and fed to the vultures. This is considered the best way to reach the heavens.

The body is never buried underground, and every trace of flesh or blood must be removed before the relatives' eyes, in order to avoid any discomfort for the deceased or his surviving family.

Ancient Justice

In times of old, the following methods of 'justice' were meted out to those unfortunate enough to incur the wrath of the law:

Drowning
The offender would be bound and thrown into a particularly dangerous part of the river, sometimes with a rock around his neck. On one such occasion the criminal was rescued by some large fish who ate through his bindings, leaving him to emerge shaken and bruised but still alive. He became a reformed character and was allowed to live in peace.

Crucifixion
The criminal would be stripped naked and tied firmly to the cross, his head held upright using his own hair. In this way the offender was not injured or wounded in any way, but would simply die of thirst, hunger, cold etc.

Boiling Oil
The offender would be thrown into a pot of boiling oil, thus avoiding any bleeding, in accordance with religious views.

Beating and Piercing
For thieves, one of the punishments was to pierce the nails with bamboo and beat the thief while he was hanging upside down. If the stolen property was not recovered, the thief would be made to walk through the town naked while he was pelted with large boulders until he died.

Brigadier Teg Bahadur Kapur writes that, "*Contrary to expectations, such painful penalties for crime acted as a strong deterrent and the area was relatively crime-free.*"

Chapter Six

FESTIVALS

Festivals are one of the highlights of a visit to Ladakh, and for the local people they provide an excuse to dress up, drink, have fun and at the same time earn religious merit. One of the most important parts of the festivals is the Cham dance. These dances are choreographed in great detail, and are performed by lamas in incredible costumes, while an orchestra of monks plays the drums, long horns and cymbals. Each of these dances has a theme, which is to show the destruction of evil and demonstrate the illusory nature of life. They also make offerings to the tutelary deities and *yidams* of each monastery.

Some of the masks are fierce, one might even say grotesque, not the sort of face you would want to meet on a dark night. Others might have the peaceful countenance of a benign Buddha. They usually represent Buddhist gods and characters from Tibetan fables. The more fierce ones normally represent guardians or protectors in their wrathful Tantric form. When not being used for the festival dances, these masks are often stored in the Gonkhang of each monastery and you may see them hanging on the pillars if you're lucky.

The dances are usually held in the courtyard of the monastery, around a specially erected flagpole. Holding sacred objects in their hands, the lamas mime to the deeply resonant sombre music that is so spiritually uplifting for them and for any listener, tourist or otherwise. To lighten the experience, in-between dances a masked jester might appear and invite one of the audience to take part in a 'clown' sequence, poking gentle fun at the unsuspecting participant and making everybody laugh.

Most of the festivals last for two days, starting on the first day with prayers for the safe proceeding of the festival. After the dances, on the second day, effigies are burnt to signify the destruction of evil spirits.

Festival dates 2014 – 2017

Name	2014	2015	2016	2017
Spituk *Gu-Stor*	Jan 28 & 29	Jan 18 & 19	Jan 7 & 8	Jan 24 & 25
Leh, Likir & Diskit *Dosmoche*	Feb 27 & 28	Feb 16 & 17	Feb 5 & 6	Feb 23 & 24
Stok *Guru Tse-Chu*	March 10 & 11	Feb 27 & 28	Feb 15 & 16	March 5 & 6
Matho *Nagrang*	March 15 & 16	March 4 & 5	Feb 22 & 23	March 12 & 13
Buddha Purnima	June 13	June 2	June 20	June 8
Hemis *Tse-Chu*	July 7 & 8	June 26 & 27	July 13 & 14	July 2 & 3
Lamayuru *Kab-Gyat*	June 24 & 25	July dates	July not	July fixed
Karsha *Gu-Stor*	July 24 & 25	July 14 & 15	July/Aug 31 & 1	July 20 & 21
Phyang *Tse-Dup*	July 24 & 25	July 14 & 15	August 1 & 2	July 20 & 21
Korzok *Gu-Stor*	July 30 & 31	July 19 & 20	August 6 & 7	July 25 & 26
Traktok *Tse-Chu*	August 6 & 7	July 26 & 27	August 12 & 13	July/Aug 31 & 1
Sani *Naro Nas-Jal*	August 9 & 10	July 30 & 31	August 16 & 17	August 4 & 5
Shashukul *Gu-Stor*	July 24 & 25	July 4 & 5	July Not	July fixed
Thikse *Gu-Stor*	Nov 9 & 10	Oct 30 & 31	Nov 16 & 17	Nov 5 & 6
Chemrey *Wangchok*	Nov 20 & 21	Nov 9 &10	Nov 26 & 27	Nov 14 & 15
Galdan Namchot	Dec 15	Dec 4	Dec 21	Dec 10
Losar	Dec 22	Dec 12	Dec 29	Dec 16
Ladakh Festival	**Varies**	**each**	**year**	

Tibetan Calendar

Based on the lunar year, the Tibetan calendar consists of twelve months of thirty days each, in theory. To make this match up with the solar year of 365¼ days, an extra month is added every third year. This is not added at any fixed point, but at an auspicious time determined by an astrologer. Another problem is that the actual lunar year is made up of only 354 days, not the theoretical 360 days, so further adjustments have to be made by cutting out certain days. Other days may be repeated, just adding to the confusion.

The actual Tibetan year begins in February or March, with the new moon. The months have no names, only numbers one to twelve, but the days of the week are named after the planets, and the years are named after animals, repeating every twelve years. And in 1027AD, a sixty-year cycle was introduced. This is made up of five cycles of twelve years, each cycle named after the five elements: wood, fire, earth, iron and water.

Because of these complications, how can you know on which dates to plan your trip in order to see one of these wondrous extravaganzas? The Tibetan calendar is traditionally only prepared at the end of each year by an astrologer, and it is not customary for the calendar to be prepared in advance.

However, this obviously makes it difficult for tourists to plan their visits to Ladakh to see these festivals, which bring in much-needed income to Ladakh. Because of this, the Jammu & Kashmir Tourist Department consult an astrologer and asked him to prepare a calendar of auspicious dates for several years ahead. The dates, where fixed for the next four years, are as shown in the table on the preceding page. Dates shown in the chart for the festivals may vary by a couple of days.

For more details, see
www.jktourism.org
www.ladakh-tourism.net/Ladakh_Festivals.htm
www.ratnavoyages.com/monastic-festivals-2014

Main festivals of Ladakh

Gu-Stor *commemorating the victory of good over evil*

Literally this means 'sacrifice of the 9th day'. It starts with the
Ser-kyem offering to the gods, inviting them to attend the
sacred dances. The festival lasts two days, during which time
the lamas dance wearing the masks of the Dharmapala
guardians and patron saints of the Gelug-pa sect. On the last
day a human figure made from dough is 'sacrificed', being
dismembered with ritual weapons; this process is known as
Dao-Tulva, killing of the enemy. The pieces are then thrown
away in all four cardinal directions, symbolising the
banishment of all enemies as well as the assassination of King
Langdarma by a Buddhist monk (see History). Later in the day
another effigy, **Stor-ma**, symbolising even stronger evil forces,
is burnt with great celebration.

Dosmoche *the great winter festival*

This is the last event of the New Year celebrations, and occurs
every February. It was instituted by the kings of Ladakh to
imitate the Monlam festival of Lhasa in Tibet. The main event
consists of sacred dances in the courtyard below Leh Palace.
Lamas come from all over Ladakh to take part, chosen in
rotation, but it is only lamas from Traktok who are specialised
enough to make the 'Do', an intricate cross-thread model
which is believed to trap evil spirits, ghosts and demons when
it has been consecrated. Ten other offerings are added to this,
and all are carried down through the town in a great
procession in which townspeople and monks take part, with
the monastic orchestra beating drums, blowing horns and
clashing cymbals as they proceed. At the end of town the
offerings are burnt and the 'Do' is overturned. All the
participants chant prayers, wishing away all evil spirits and
praying for peace and protection throughout the following year.

Similar Dosmoche festivals take place at Likir and Diskit.

Tse-Chu *Padma Sambhava's birthday*

The 10th day of every Tibetan month is considered auspicious, and in particular, those of the 5th and 10th months are considered especially so, being celebrated as the birthday of Guru Rinpoche, otherwise known as Padma Sambhava.

The festival at Hemis is particularly famous, being two hundred years old. The costumes represent mainly deities of the Druk-pa. In essence, the Hemis dances show the eight forms of Padma Sambhava vanquishing the enemies of Buddhism and ensuring its survival and growth. He is revered for having tamed and converted the pre-Buddhist Bon deities to Buddhism. Every twelve years the Hemis festival is even more special, as a two-storey-high thangka of Padma Sambhava is unveiled. It is elaborately embroidered and studded with pearls and precious stones. It was last shown in 2004, so it's not long to wait for the next time. The Hemis festival was started as a summer festival right from the beginning, unlike most others, which began in the winter months but have now switched to the summer.

Tse-Chu is also celebrated at the only Nyingma-pa monastery in the region that of Traktok, as well as Stok, in fact at the small attached monastery of Gurphug.

Matho Nagrang *festival of the oracles*

This is a unique festival, held only at Matho. Two monks go into a trance, becoming the protector Rongtsen Kar Mar. Oracles predict events, running along the walls and rooftops blindfold, cutting themselves with knives and nails. The following morning they are found to show no signs of the damage inflicted the day before; no scars nor bleeding remain. This truly amazing feat inspires admiration from the local crowd and tourists.

Phyang Tse-Dup *displaying special thangka*

This festival includes more colourful dances and votive offerings, as well the display of the special ancient thangka of Skyabje Jigten Gombo, founder of the Drigung-pa, which is unveiled only once every three years. Thousands of Ladakhis come from all over the region, as well as many foreign tourists.

Lamayuru Yuru Kab-Gyat

A two-day festival held at Lamayuru; the dances and masks here represent the Drigung-pa traditions.

Losar *New Year*

The Ladakhi New Year is celebrated two months earlier than in other Tibetan communities. This has happened since the 16th century, when King Jamyang Namgyal had to lead a winter expedition into enemy territory, and was advised by his astrologer that it would be unwise to do so without celebrating the New Year first. See History for more information.

The most important of Ladakhi celebrations, Losar consists of a complex mix of Bon and Buddhist rituals. Once the harvest is over, people start to stock up for the festival, with grain, sheep and goats. People also like to have new clothes and jewellery. Muslims in Ladakh also follow this tradition.

On New Year's Day itself, people make offerings at the shrines of their own personal gods, visiting relatives and friends, presenting gifts and the white scarves known as *khata* (as in Nepal). Muslims and Christians also take part in this tradition, offering these gifts and khata to their Buddhist friends.

Another popular custom is to make drawings of ibex on walls, doors and columns. The ibex is regarded as symbol of fertility and prosperity for the family. Models of ibex are also moulded from dough and placed on kitchen shelves.

At the end of the celebrations, processions of people march through the town carrying flaming torches, which are waved through the air, creating fantastic patterns of fire and light. They chant prayers to scare away the ghosts and evil spirits that have built up over the year because of the bad karma and wrongdoing of the people. In conclusion, the flaming torches are thrown away, symbolising the end of the old year and the start of a new beginning.

Galdan Namchot *Tsong Khapa's birthday*

This celebrates the birthday and Buddhahood of Tsong Khapa, the founder of the Gelug-pa sect. It is an important social as well as religious festival. All public and residential buildings are illuminated, as well as the monasteries. Marking the start of the season of the New Year festivities, every household prepares the traditional Ladakhi food of 'thukpa', a hearty soup, to serve to visiting guests.

Ladakh festival

Celebrated at the beginning of September every year, this date is the only one not fixed by astrologers. It is organised by the state tourist organisation, J&K Tourism, with help from the local authorities. Its aim is to promote Ladakh's rich cultural heritage to the rest of the world. Processions, orchestras, folk dances and archery, along with monastic masked dance-drama performances, all continue throughout this two-week-long festival of colour and culture.

Gyaji puja: to bless one's home and family

Our first visits to Leh had been in the summers from 1977 through to 1984. In 2006, we visited for the first time during the winter. It was the end of January, and we were just beginning to come to terms with the freezing cold weather and the breathtaking altitude. A newborn calf shivered in the living room of our guesthouse and was shown into the kitchen to warm itself by the fire. We were more than happy to do the same!

In the corner of the living room, the oracle was preparing herself. First wrapping an elaborate headdress around her head, she then began loud and vigorous chanting, violently shaking a bell in her left hand and twirling a drum in her right hand.

This went on for about half an hour, as she worked her way into a trance. Once she had finished this performance, the family members presented her with prayer flags and began a discussion; this appeared to be a form of fortune telling, with very serious faces all round.

It seemed as though the activities might go on all day, and we had so many monasteries to seek out and discover, so we left as the uncle of the family came to prepare what looked like hundreds of tiny butter lamps. Later in the day we returned to find the table of 108 (an auspicious number) butter lamps ablaze with colour and warmth.

In another corner sat a man who had previously been a monk but had then served in the Indian Army and was now retired. He sat alone, chanting and beating a large drum, smiling at us as we walked into the room. The butter lamps had been arranged in a square mandala. Outside the square were effigies of 'witches', like candles of flour and butter, some with wicks and others without. None of them were lit. These 'witches' were placed on all four sides, representing north, south, east and west. Once the ex-monk had finished his chanting, the two men of the house picked up the 'witches' and indicated to us that we should follow them outside. Carrying two trays each, one turned left and the other right outside the gate. The 'witches' were unceremoniously dumped into the ditch on the side of the road.

And thus were the bad spirits of the four directions disposed of.

Chapter Seven

LEH

Leh lies at a breath-taking altitude of 3505m. In recent years the town has expanded considerably, to the south, north and west. The principal thoroughfare remains the street south of the large main mosque. Further south, bazaars, shops and colourful markets now extend well south of the old town's confines, marked by a very tall square-based stupa. Over the road is a new Tibetan-style arched gate. Heading south down the hill on the right is a large mani wall that hosts shops and bazaars on each side.

The main bus station lies at the bottom of this market, on the right. The road now continues south past the hospital to a large roundabout. From here roads fan out to the airport, Spituk and beyond to the northwest; to the southeast is the road to Choglamsar, Shey, Hemis and Manali. Northwest of the town is the settlement of Changspa, where old chortens vie with new guesthouses. All are set below Shanti Stupa, a modern attraction but no less imposing for that.

North of the town is the area known as Chubi (or Chube), which has sprouted a lot of new guesthouses among the trees and fields. Here is the significant monastery of Shankar, which should not be missed. It is possible to climb up to the old Tsemo fort high above the palace on a path from the north here. It's a pleasant walk, given some acclimatisation to altitude.

There are three mosques; the main mosque, which is green and on the corner of the main street, is not as old as the two smaller ones close by.

Map of monasteries in the Leh area

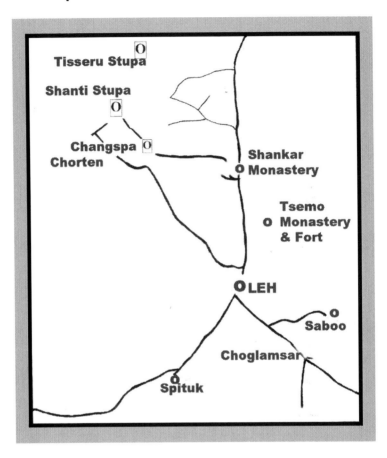

Chokhang (Jokhang)

In the central part of Leh, off the main street to the west, is the large courtyard of the Chokhang complex. The central three-tiered Tibetan pagoda-style temple was consecrated by the Dalai Lama on 06 September 1980. There are eighty-nine prayer wheels around the building, which apparently send millions of 'Om Mani Padme Hum' prayers skywards. Inside, the central deity is the Sakyamuni Buddha, with Guru Rinpoche to his right. Also visible are three thrones; one is set aside for the Dalai Lama. The decoration inside is fairly simple, but the place attracts many devoted followers. In February a 10-day series of prayers were being held, with horns, drums and symbols played by monks. In the courtyard is the office of the Ladakhi Buddhist Association and some new and older-style buildings.

Central Mosque

Standing below the Palace at the north end of the main street is the green-domed Jami Masjid (mosque) of the Sunni branch. It was built in the mid-17th century when King Delek Namgyal, having invited the support of the Moghul ruler Aurangzeb in a conflict, had to provide ground in recognition of this help. Taksang Raspa contributed to its decoration. Carpets came from Yarkand, as did craftsmen to make the pulpit for the Imam's lessons. It was initially a two-storey building, but has been considerably extended over the years including the addition of a bath area, the hammam, constructed in 1947. The two other mid-19th century mosques belong to the Shia branch of Islam.

Tsemo

Location
High on the hill above Leh town.

How to get there
A new road leads much of the way up from the east side. The climb from old Leh is steep and relentless. Another track leads up from the hamlet on the Khardung La road opposite the turn to Shankar. The climb takes about 20–30 minutes and the views are superb.

About the monasteries
Tsemo, which lies behind and high above the town, is a collection of chapels and a fort on Namgyal Tsemo peak. The topmost building, a white-walled crumbling structure with elaborate wooden balconies, is a former Dard fortress, parts of

which date back to the 5th century. The present structure was built under Tashi Namgyal some time between 1555 and 1575.

Two gompas, probably built by King Trags Bum-ide in 1430, stand just below the fortress ruins. Women are only allowed into the gompas when the statues are veiled. In any case, whether male or female, it is difficult to gain access to these gompas; not only are they at the top of a very steep and intimidating hill, they are also only open during the early morning and late afternoon, and then at unpredictable hours. We do not recommend attempting the hill in the dark!

The Maitreya Namgyal Tsemo Gompa is a red chapel and contains images of Avalokiteshvara, Guru Rinpoche and Sakyamuni. As the name suggests, the central deity here is Maitreya, the future Buddha.

The Gonkhang or temple of the four Lokapalas, those four familiar guarding deities, is attributed to Tashi Namgyal. Legend suggests that he built the temple around a statue of Mahakala and over the corpses of Mongol invaders, in order to deter further attacks. The Mahakala image is also worshipped by childless women for fertility.

Leh Palace and monasteries

> *The ruins of Italian castles pale in comparison with this picturesque pile, this mass which rises in the chalice of the many-coloured mountains.*
> **Altai Himalaya***: Nicholas Roerich*

Location
Leh Palace is directly north of the main street and mosque.

How to get there
By taxi the road winds around the polo ground in the new suburbs of east Leh. On foot you must take the 'street of bakeries' behind the large main mosque, then turn right under the chorten into the alleys and tunnels that zigzag up through old houses. A path then climbs steeply up to the cluster of chapels below the palace. Another route goes east from the

mosque into old houses towards a large stupa and then on to the main palace access road.

About the Palace
The imposing nine-storey Leh Palace was built by Sengge Namgyal in the 16th century. It took three years to complete and was burnt down in 1685 by the Tibetans and Mongolians. Much of the design is attributed to a Balti Muslim, Chanden Ali Sengge.

At the entrance is a large wooden door with three guarding snow lions sitting above. Chalden Ali Sengge was responsible for these images, the top one of which can be moved in or out. Visitors enter at the fourth level, with its various welcoming halls. The ground area was used as stables. The second floor was used for storage and the third was used by the servants. The fifth floor housed the King's Audience hall, the Tsokhang.

On the sixth floor were king and queen's private areas. The seventh floor houses the image of Dukkar, known as the lady with a white parasol, and also a thousand-armed aspect of Tara. The Samyeling Lhakhang has some Gelug-pa images, as well as Tara, Sakyamuni, Palden Lhamo, the fierce female Tibetan deity, and Guru Rinpoche. The eighth floor comprises of seven rooms of unknown use, and the top level, the ninth, has a prayer room.

Below the palace on the south side are a number of chapels currently under restoration, some involving Tibetan refugee finances.

Leh Palace

Leh Palace area

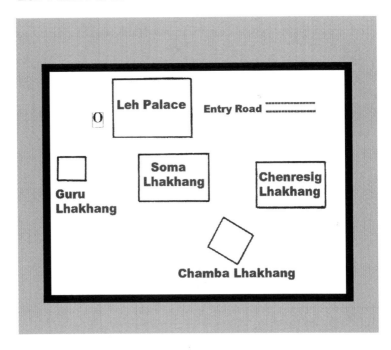

Chenresig Lhakhang

This large, ancient white chapel, located just below the Leh Palace road, is unusual in that it has two doorways, on the east and west sides. The structure was erected by King Tsepal, the last effective ruler of the Namgyal dynasty, around 1815. It is dedicated to Avalokiteshvara, whose image appears at the east end. The image, which is standing, has eight arms. To the right side is a thangka painting, with the altar in front of the main deity. On the walls are fading images of the Buddha; set in six lines these small images number in the thousands. On each side are found four larger Buddha images. In the roof atrium are some protector images. There are several books and on the west wall the Lokapalas stand guard.

Leh Chenresig Lhakhang

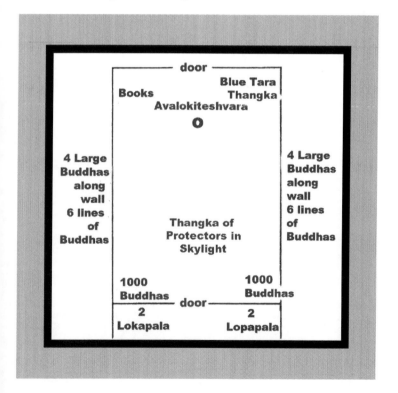

Chamba Lhakhang

This tall, squat structure houses an impressive image of Maitreya. It was built in the early 15th century; if the wooden doors are locked you can peer through the cracks of the wooden doors to see much of the image. It is flanked by two equally impressive but much smaller orange-coloured statues. It is located below Chenresig Lhakhang.

Soma Lhakhang

The Soma Lhakhang is a larger chapel west of Chenresig Lhakhang. It has some unusual art forms. On the east wall are some Chinese-looking paintings with a Guru Rinpoche and Mahakala image each side. The main devotional deities are Guru Rinpoche on the right of the Sakyamuni Buddha. An image called Tangri Mahakala sits by the east wall. To the left is a marble Avalokiteshvara. On the west wall are further paintings, of animals, leopards, ducks and lions. A strange boat and some Chinese letters also grace the wall. As you enter there is an image of Vajrapani to the left of the doorway. The four guarding Lokapalas can also be seen before entering.

Soma Lhakhang

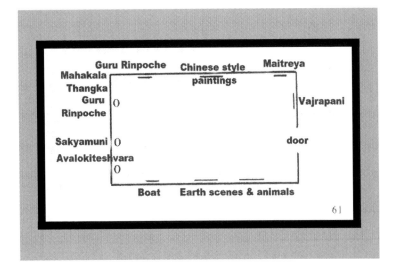

69

Guru Lhakhang

This chapel is almost restored and is found to the extreme west of the complex of shrines below the palace. It sits just below the imposing chorten that dominates the scene of the palace. It is rather hard to access; you need to scramble up through the alleys of old Leh near the mosque. Inside is a tall vision of Guru Rinpoche.

Closer to Old Leh and the mosque is a new chapel called Kurgon Gompa, which may be closed in winter. Nearby, just slightly uphill to the west, is the House of Norchung Hanupa and Domkhapa. The Tibetan Heritage Fund, with donations from the Tibetan community, is helping to restore some of the sites below the palace. The alleyways down to the main street have been concreted underfoot to make access easier. An ancient crumbling chorten sits above the entrance tunnel in the street of bakeries.

The last sign from Leh was the farewell of the women of Ladakh. They went out on the road carrying the blessed milk of yaks. They sprinkled the milk on the foreheads of the horses and travellers in order to give them the power of yaks, so needed on the steep inclines and upon the slippery ribs of the glaciers. The women bade us farewell... And above us stood snow-covered Khardung! It rose unapproachably.
Altai Himalaya: *Nicholas Roerich*

Leh from Shanti Stupa
70

Around Leh

Shanti Stupa

Location
The latest addition to the Leh skyline is the white Shanti Stupa, set on a hill to the west of Leh Palace. The hill, some 100m or more high, is reached after a pleasant 30-minute walk through the western lanes of Leh and into Changspa village. Many new guesthouses dot the fields here. See list in Chapter 12.

How to get there
Approaching from the south you may take a staircase of 566 steps to reach the main level. On the way up are two sets of chortens. Road access is long, via a circuitous route north of Leh. A further nineteen steps lead on to the main stupa plinth, which has sweeping vistas all around. The views of Leh are superb, as are the mountains of the Ladakh range to the north.

About the stupa
The stupa itself has two accessible levels. Adorning the lower circuit are fifty-three Buddha images, and above are four images depicting the life cycle. On the east is the 'wheel of dharma'; to the south is the reclining Buddha among dancing apsara-like figures – the 'maharani nirvana.' On the west side is the birth zone with a standing Buddha, and to the north are scenes of the defeating of devils, with a sitting Buddha. In between we see fourteen Buddhas in classic position between the four directional images.

Below the stupa is a small chapel, the Shanti Gompa. A golden Buddha adorns the main altar, with a golden stupa above and some thangkas decorating the room. A Wheel of Life held by a red Yama sits to the left of the smaller Buddha figures. Drums on each side accompany the scene here.

Changspa Stupa
North of Leh Palace, in the village of Changspa and beyond, are two ancient chortens or stupas. In the village, standing in a shady grove of trees, is a mandala-shaped chorten. This is

Changspa Stupa; it has many Buddha images in its encircling niches. There is a cattle-breeding farm close to Shanti Stupa, selling fresh milk through a hole in the wall.

Changspa Stupa

Stupa of Tiserru

Further north, well clear of the town, are the ancient mud brick ruins of the Tiserru Stupa, a large diameter complex. The complex dates from the 14th century. Its central tower has crumbled over the centuries, but it is believed to have had 108 chapels. It is clearly visible from the Shanti Stupa hill. This stupa must have been gigantic once.

Shankar (Gelug-pa)

Location
Shankar (Sankar) Monastery is located across fields in a residential area 2km northwest of Leh.

How to get there
Apart from taking a taxi from Leh, it can be reached in two ways. Firstly by following the Khardung La road, then heading left along the Shankar road and taking a right then a left to the north gate. A more traditional route is to head west towards the

new communications tower, left off Shankar road, then head further west to find the chorten and stupa pathway to the south gate of the monastery.

Accommodation
There is a wealth of choice in guesthouses close by. See appendix.

About the monastery
If you come to Shankar from the south you will pass a large stupa topped with a red spire. Here are some stone tablets depicting Buddhist images. A little further on is a shrine known in Tibetan as the 'Rigsum Gonpo', meaning 'Protectors of the three realms'. High up on the north side are three protectors displayed in paintings behind three chortens. They are Manjushri, Avalokiteshvara and Vajrapani.

Shankar Monastery

The monastery is part of the Spituk domain and belongs to the reformist Gelug-pa sect of Tsong Khapa. The main dukhang is entered from the north side of the rectangular monastic quarters set around a pleasant garden area. A staircase leads to the entrance. On the right is an image of the old man of longevity, sometimes called Mi Gan. He is like the Mi Tsering goblin figure of Buddhists in Nepal.

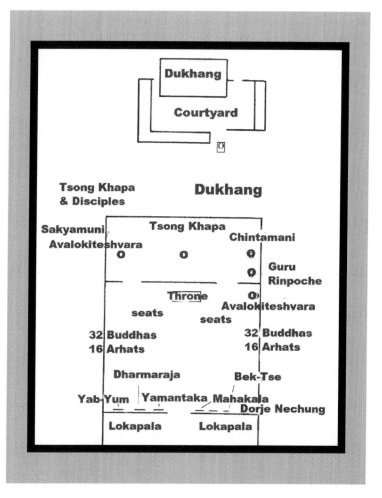

Inside, along the walls are the sixteen arhats, and twice as many benevolent Buddha images. A central Sakyamuni is flanked by a striking image of Avalokiteshvara. A rather unusual deity here is the white Mahakala, called Chintamani, in the right corner. Dukkar, a deity of one thousand heads, arms and legs, is displayed at the back. Also seen here are Guru Rinpoche (Padma Sambhava) and Tsong Khapa.

74

Mobile Monks

How do you send a text message when your fingers are frozen solid? Ask a young monk in a Ladakhi monastery!

Many was the time we would be puzzling over the name of a particularly beautiful or intriguing icon, only to ask the teenage monk accompanying us and find him entranced by the minutely intricate piece of technology in his hand.

In years gone by, perhaps, a mobile monk might have been one who went to Tibet to study and then came back to Ladakh to practise. The only texts in the monasteries would have been written on ancient parchment.

Nowadays, every young monk will have a mobile phone glued to his ear or hand, as he is mesmerised by the new technology. Or his fingers will be typing away on his keyboard, sending text messages to his nearest and dearest, or perhaps searching for the football results?

Chapter Eight

SOUTHEAST OF LEH

Stok

Location
14km from Leh, Stok lies on a hilltop almost due south of Leh, on the opposite side of the Indus river.

How to get there
This is one of the easiest to visit by public bus, which is of course very cheap. If you go by taxi, you could visit two or three monasteries as part of the same day out.

Accommodation
None. See under Leh.

About the monastery
Stok was built by Tsepal Namgyal around 1820. He was effectively the last of the Namgyal kings to exercise real power. After the Dogra invasion of 1834, Stok became the royal residence. The name of the structure and the village is derived from a word describing the apex of a gilded stupa.

Like so many Ladakhi monasteries, it is spectacularly situated on a hilltop, with a 360-degree panoramic view of the Zanskar range to the south and the Ladakh range to the north.

At present the current Queen of Ladakh uses the palace; she is a descendant of Kunzang Namgyal. The building hosts a stupa with some of the remains of Tsepal Namgyal inside. Stok Palace is now a museum and library. The fine collection of books here includes versions of the Tibetan Holy Scriptures, the Kangyur.

It is only open during the summer season.
See www.stokpalace.com.

Map of monasteries southeast of Leh

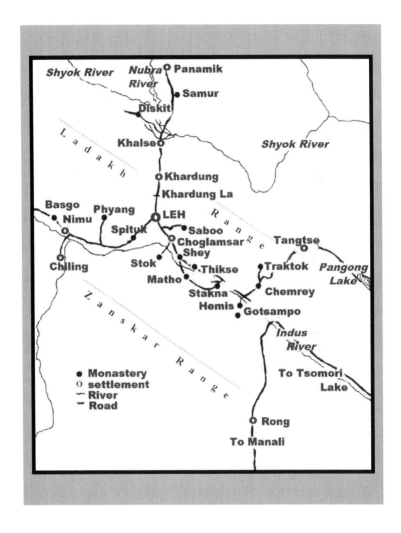

Saboo (Sabu)

Location
8km from Leh, Saboo is hidden from view until the last minute and almost impossible to photograph because of the trees and hills in the way. The monastery lies further uphill beyond the village.

How to get there
Take a taxi from Leh; it is very close. There may be a public bus if you're lucky, but the taxi is inexpensive. By taxi you could visit two or three monasteries as part of the same day out.

Accommodation
None. Try Leh or the outlying Tibetan refugee village of Choglamsar.

About the monastery
A small monastery with two main chapels, we were unable to see the inside because the head lama or the man-with-the-key was in Leh, a common tale if you go out of season. Narrow lanes connect the buildings. It is said to contain a superb Avalokiteshvara with eleven heads, a large Sakyamuni and Padma Sambhava.

Nearby are the ruins of the old castle tower of Sengge Namgyal.

Choglamsar

Location
About 6km from Leh on the Hemis road, it is a rapidly expanding settlement.

How to get there
A taxi is very fast and minibuses run regularly throughout the day.

Accommodation
Some basic guesthouses; try Indus Guesthouse or Buddha Garden Guesthouse.

About the town
Choglamsar is the main centre for Tibetan refugees and is now rapidly being developed with government buildings and new complexes. On the left of the main road from Leh is a vast mani wall and chortens. The name derives from two words, Chok and Tsel.

Shey

Location
15km from Leh, on the south face of a hillside, with the old fortress above it further along the ridge top.

How to get there
This is one of the easiest to visit by public bus, which is of course very cheap. If you go by taxi, you could visit two or three monasteries as part of the same day out.

Accommodation
Try the Shilkar Hotel or Bestung Guesthouse. Otherwise stay in Leh or the outlying Tibetan refugee village of Choglamsar.

About the monastery
Shey was once the capital of Ladakh; the old fortress is now in ruins. There are some impressive engraved Dhyani Buddhas on the rock on the corner of the road below the ridge. Before entering the complex it is recommended to explore the ridge top to the south, where a number of recently restored chortens are set decorated with many prayer flags. To the northwest is the large mandala-style stupa reminiscent of such structures found at Toling in Tibet.

Within the old palace is a two-storey temple with a seated gilded Buddha inside, commissioned by Sengge Namgyal. The main chapel houses a large Sakyamuni Buddha and the two-storied structure around it was executed by Deldan Namgyal around 1633 as a funeral memorial to his father Sengge Namgyal. Guru Rinpoche, Palden Lhamo, the sixteen arhats and Chakpa Maylen are the main idols on display.

Another chapel is supposedly devoted to Amitayus, the Buddha of Longevity, and was probably constructed by Queen Kalzang, the Balti wife of Sengge Namgyal.

There are also an incredible number of white chortens on the south side of the road beyond Shey village. Ranging from large and small, single and linked, these white crumbling blobs number in the thousands. The site has apparently been used for several film sets, both Hollywood and Bollywood. A kilometre out of the village on the way to Thikse is Naropa Pothang, the house of the head lama of Hemis, set back across the fields near the chortens.

Shey – Main (Sakyamuni) Lhakhang

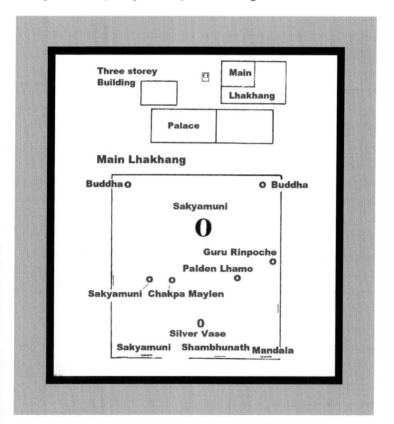

Thikse (Gelug-pa)

Location
19km southeast of Leh, Thikse is one of the most photographed monasteries in Ladakh. It stands proudly on top of a huge hill, with hundreds of steps for the visitor to climb up, literally taking one's breath away even before entering the amazing chapels.

How to get there
This is one of the easiest to visit by public bus, which is of course very cheap (Rs20 single). If you go by taxi, you could visit two or three monasteries as part of the same day out.

Accommodation
Chamba Guesthouse and Restaurant in summer.

About the monastery
Thikse is one of the most famous of all of Ladakh's monasteries. Its gleaming white buildings climb up the steep-sided hill of its location to a summit of superb red, yellow and white chapels. It was founded in the mid-15th century by two emissaries of Tsong Khapa: the sage, Sherab Zangpo, and his disciple, Spon Palden Sherab.

The current reincarnate is Nawang Chamba Stenzin. He was born in 1943 at Chushot village near the monastery. His education took place at Drepung and Tashi Lhunpo in Tibet. He also developed the monastic schools at Thikse and at Diskit in the Nubra valley, as well as being the power behind the construction of the Chamba Lhakhang. He is a Member of Parliament. At present there are almost 100 monks studying at Thikse.

It is believed that the great translator Rinchen Zangpo built a chapel here in the 11th century, a building that can no longer be seen. What remains today are a number of chapels; the old Dukhang, the Gonkhang, and the latest and much-admired addition, the red Chamba Lhakhang of Maitreya on the east end. Other chapels include the Kudung Lhakhang and the Dolma Lhakhang.

Thikse Monastery

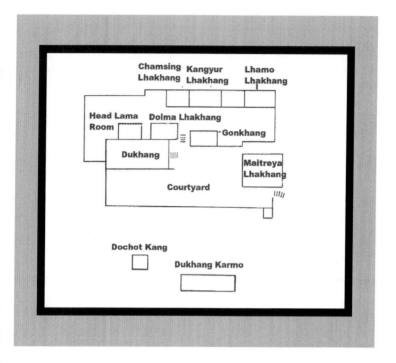

From the car park area, you head past some ageing chortens to the foot of the hill and, following a new stairway, climb past a large chorten then a row of seven or eight smaller chortens. Here on the wall are some figures of peacocks, horses and snow lions, as well as some bodhisattvas. The large white chapel is to your right as you climb to the throne of the lamas. The path divides – either way will take you to the main courtyard; the right path goes under a tunnel to this place.

The most imposing sight at Thikse is the 12m (40ft) high golden statue of Maitreya. This is the image that appears in most promotional literature; it was built in 1979. Maitreya is in a sitting position, wearing a golden crown. Behind and on the sides are images of Tsong Khapa and Sakyamuni. The Dolma Lhakhang is a chapel containing images of the twenty-one

Taras, Namgyal-ma, Kachokma, Vajrapani, Dorje Sempa and Chenresig, as well as Tsong Khapa.

Thikse Monastery

In the Kudung Lhakhang, the newest of Thikse's chapels, are two large silver and gold stupas. The 6th reincarnate Nawang Namgyal and the seventh, Chamba Sokmit, are on display here, as well as the current 9th incumbent head lama. A new yab-yum painting adorns one of the walls. Two new images were awaiting painting, these being a complex five-headed yab-yum with the consort having two heads – Chakra Sambhava or Demchok – and the other, also a yab-yum, is Tsangdu. Both are awaiting transfer to the Old Dukhang.

Often closed, on the roof are two further chapels. The Lhamo Lhakhang is on the north side, presumably housing a statue of Palden Lhamo, the fierce female deity. Next to it is the Kangyur or book chapel. The other room is the Chamsing Lhakhang, which contains images of Chamsing and Palden Lhamo.

Maitreya Lhakhang

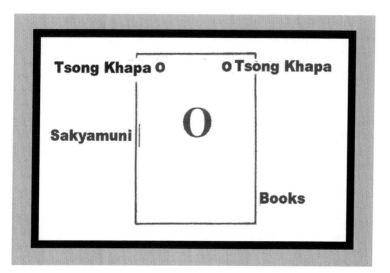

Dolma Lhakhang

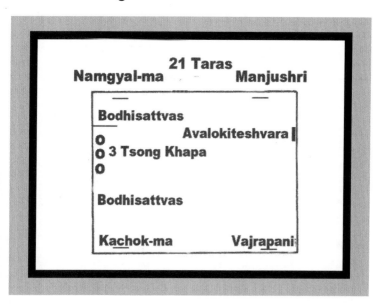

The larger chapel of the old dukhang, sometimes referred to as the Nyingma Lhakhang, has some very imposing images. Some of these include Demchok, a deity closely associated with Mount Kailash. Another is Tsangdu, commonly known in Sanskrit as Guhyasamaja, linked to the Tantric scriptures bearing the same name.

Perhaps the most astonishing chapel is the gonkhang, where the ferocious mind-curdling protectors are gathered in a dark and solemn temple, disturbed only by a lone monk beating a drum in near total blackness, an eerie song to the dead. Hidden in this ghostly chamber are Kitapala, a strange veiled idol with spiky crown and skulls, sitting on an even stranger vehicle – a beast defying description. A two-headed Yamantaka is the tallest central deity. He is not veiled, his mouth is menacingly open, and his eyes drift upwards. He holds a vajra, is black and holds many skulls. A four-armed Mahakala sits to the right. On the left is Kala Repa, the black-clad one; both are veiled. This chapel was said to be one thousand years old, which might tie in with the lost chamber of Rinchen Zangpo. This current chamber is around five hundred years old.

Thikse

Thikse Dukhang

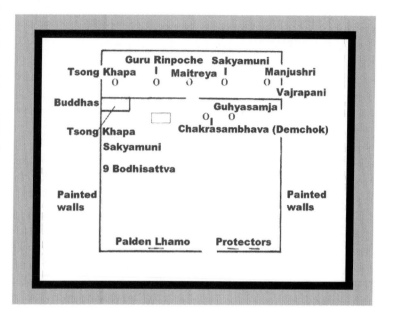

Thikse Gonkhang

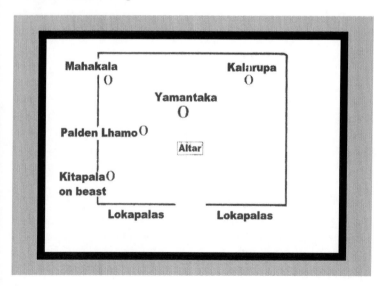

Nyar-ma

This monastery, which is completely in ruins, is close to Thikse on the plains. Its existence is noted in an inscription at Alchi, and it is closely linked to Rinchen Zangpo. A fort originally protected it from dangers.

Matho (Sakya-pa)

Location
Matho is situated on top of a small hill 26km southeast of Leh, on the south side of the valley, jutting out from the higher mountains behind. It is a small place and a tour there should probably be combined with a visit to other monasteries in this part of the valley.

How to get there
There is unlikely to be any public transport. Take a taxi. Don't consider hitching unless you have unlimited time. A road runs parallel to the main Thikse–Hemis route to the south which links Stakna to Matho.

Accommodation
None.

About the monastery
Founded in the 15th century by the Tibetan Sakya scholar Dorje Palsang, the land for this monastery was given by King Dragpa Bunde (Grags Bum-Ide) of Ladakh. It is the only Sakya-pa monastery in Ladakh. In the late 16th century the monastery was almost destroyed by invading Muslim forces, and the king was imprisoned. Later he was released, and the Sakya Lama Chokyi Lodo took charge of the monastery. It was common for monks from here to go to Tibet to study, and then return to Matho to practise their newfound knowledge and pass it on to young monks.

There are both old and new temples here. A special shrine houses the entire Buddhist canon; another shrine is in honour of Lamdre Lamos and there are two shrines for the protectors of the Dharma.

Matho Monastery

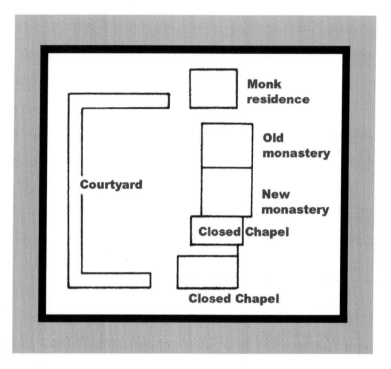

One of the greatest Sakya exponents, Sakya Pandit, who negotiated with the Mongolian overlords of Tibet at that time, is remembered within the monastery. Much of the monastery is of recent construction but nonetheless it presents a pleasing appearance. As for entry to its chapels, this can be difficult out of season. We failed miserably.

Also nearby is the cave where Dorje Palsang meditated when he first arrived here. Dorje Palsang is said to have aided in the construction of the images of Maitreya, Manjushri and Vajrapani at Matho.

The **festival** here is held in February/March. See Festivals.

Matho Monastery

Stakna (Druk-pa)

Location
25km southeast of Leh, Stakna is situated on top of a small hill on the south side of the valley above the Indus river, jutting out from the higher mountains behind. It is a small place and a tour there should probably be combined with a visit to other monasteries in this part of the valley.

How to get there
There is unlikely to be any public transport, though you could take us a bus beyond Thikse and walk from the main road, which is around 3km away. The road crosses an exciting bridge, so narrow that cars have to pull in their wing mirrors to cross it. A taxi is the best option. Don't consider hitching unless you have unlimited time.

About the monastery
The Stakna monastery first appears in chronicles of Ladakh that link it to Tsong Khapa. It is said that Shenrap Zangpo might have established some sort of monastery here. He is also believed to have been instrumental in the development of Karsha Monastery in Zanskar, as well as Diskit in Nubra. Stag

89

or *Stak* means tiger, *na* is nose, and it has links to Sengge Namgyal. It is thought the monastery dates from around 1580, which might suggest his father Jamyang Namgyal instigated its consecration. By Ladakhi standards the monastery is modest, but it commands an astonishing panorama. To the south the jagged ridges of the Zanskar range loom high. To the north the more rounded Ladakh range hints at the even greater majesty of the Karakoram further north.

Stakna Monastery

The monastery has two main chapels; the dukhang hosts some lesser-known deities. Central is the Shabdrung Nawang Namgyal, the Bhutanese senior deity who is venerated throughout Bhutan as the founder of the Druk-pa sect. He is flanked by two Bhutanese lamas and Stakpe Palzang, Tashi Tsampel on the left and Guru Rinpoche on the right. An image of Naropa, the India mystic saint, sits in front. On the east wall are images of the Buddha and one of Trisong Detsun, the Tibetan king. Close by is Kenpo Bhotia. Some newer paintings illustrate the protective deities in wrathful pose. A vision of Avalokiteshvara sits almost hidden to the left of the main deities, with Dorje Phagmo and the Shabdrung close by.

Stakna Shabdrung

Stakna Monastery

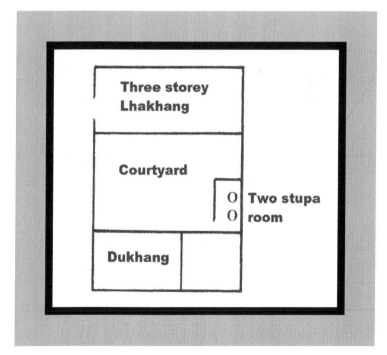

Stakna Dukhang

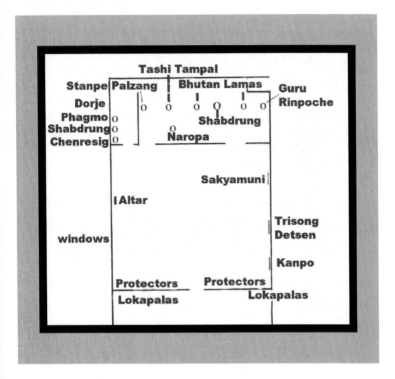

The adjacent stupa room houses two large chortens and some new and old figures. The Shabdrung again takes an important position on the right with an unknown image in the centre and a red hat lama on the left, name unknown. Some arhats adorn the walls and some old wooden stupa models are found here.

The other main chapel, a three-storied construction opposite, was closed.

Hemis (Druk-pa Kagyu-pa)

Location
45km to the southeast of Leh, it lies nestled in a valley hidden from view until the last minute, clinging to the side of the steep hillside.

How to get there
There is said to be one bus per day during the summer season. Otherwise, take a bus to the nearby village of Karu, then either hitch or take a taxi from there. The current taxi fare is quoted at Rs1050, which could include Shey and Thikse.

Accommodation
None.

About the monastery
Hemis is perhaps the most famous monastery in Ladakh. It is said to house five hundred monks, and there are at least five chambers worth a visit. Many years ago Nicholas Notovitch reported that there were documents proving that Jesus Christ had passed this way two thousand years ago, but these documents apparently no longer exist. (See History and Bibliography).

The monastery was built in the 1630s by Kushokq Shambhu Nath, the first Stagsang Raspa (Taksang Respa), and the Raj Guru of Gyalpo Singay Namgyal. After 1730, Gyalsang Rinpoche, the third incarnate Kushokq Stagsang Raspa, extended the gompa, building more shrines, chapels and stupas, with fine scriptures and murals.

The supreme head of the monastery, and the Druk-pa Kagyu-pa school of Mahayana, is His Holiness Gyalwang Dugchen. The Druk-pa school was established in the 13th century. A great sage meditated in a cave about 2km above the gompa; this cave, Gotsampo, is now a pilgrimage site, and a visit makes a pleasant walk in summer.

It is particularly noted for its colourful **festival** during June or July (the 10th and 11th day of the 5th Tibetan month), when around fifty thousand visitors descend on Leh, stretching its limited tourist resources. Some of the Cham dances include the banishing of Langdarma, the Bon King. Every twelve years a large thangka depicting Guru Rinpoche is unrolled and draped down the walls of the dukhang.

Hemis Monastery

From the courtyard where the dances take place, one can see a line of prayer wheels below the main plinth. The two main chapels here, with large entry doorways, are the Dukhang on the left and the Tsokhang on the right.

Hemis Monastery

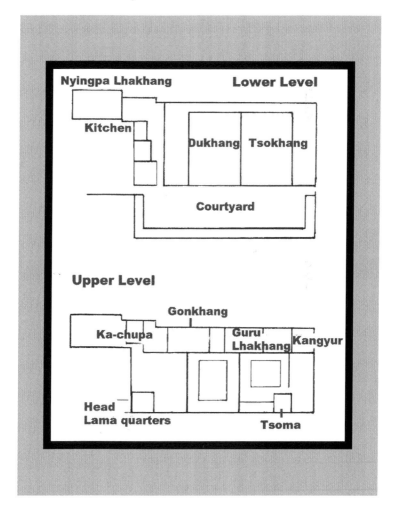

The dukhang, sometimes called the Dukhang Parpa, houses a large image of the Sakyamuni Buddha in front of a chorten. He is flanked by three chortens (one in mandala design) and a dazzling array of deities. To the left are Tara and Kushak; to the right are Suke Dorje (the second incarnation of Taksang Raspa), Takpo Laje, Amitayus and Dorje Chang. Nearer the front are Guru Rinpoche and Chintamani. Books line the right wall and the whole chamber has an evocative air.

Hemis Dukhang

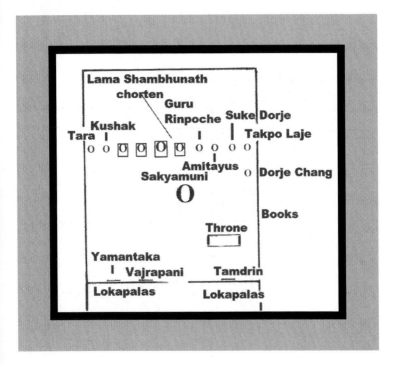

Hemis Tsokhang

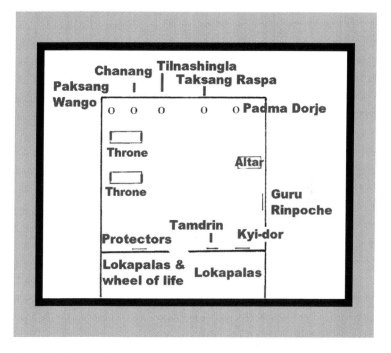

The Tsokhang has a series of lesser-known images at the rear. These include some of the former incarnates of the Rinpoche, such as Paksang Wango, Zilchok Chanang, Tilnarsingla, Padma Dorje and the head lama, Taksang Raspa. A grotesque vision of the Dharmapala protector features on the right of the main deities and closer to the exit are Kyedorje, Tamdrin and other yab-yum protectors.

Stairs lead up on to the roof, where one may view a couple of glass-windowed chambers set in small open courtyards. Also here are the Tsoma Lhakhang, which is being moved, and the new Guru Lhakhang with its 7–8m high Guru Rinpoche and colourful paintings. Also in this area is Ka Chupa Lhakhang. This small chamber has a fine Arya Avalokiteshvara on the right and books on the left. The deities here according to the monks are Dorje Sempa, Tangtong Gyalpo, Dorje Chang and

Cho Lokeshvara. The head lama's private residence is in the newly painted chapel overlooking the courtyard.

Moving downstairs on the southern end you come to a dull mud-walled chapel that appears insignificant. This is the Lhakhang Nyingpa, the oldest temple here, with a beautiful painting of the white Dorje Sempa and exquisite Kashmiri-style paintings on the rear wall. Taksang Raspa, the bearded white-hatted image, is central with Tara. Maitreya is close by. The blue-green image is Dorje Chang, with crossed arms and two vajras (dorjes). This chapel is around five hundred years old.

Hemis Nyingpa Lhakhang

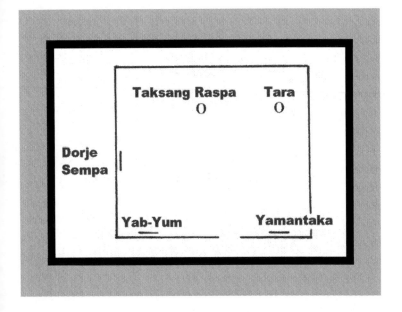

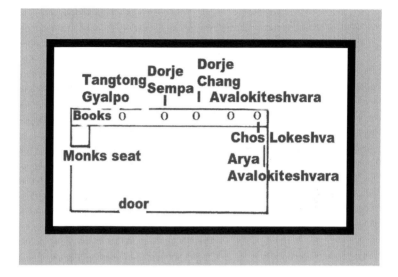

Gotsampo

The hermit retreat of Gotsampo lies up a steep track some 2–3km southwest of Hemis, further up the same rugged valley. To locate the monastery one must head south past the two schools of Hemis to a series of imposing new stupas. The path climbs steadily to an old stupa before turning to the west. Two steep-sided hanging valleys loom on the east. The path continues through the trees and crosses a stream before making a tortuous climb to the hermitage.

Whether the retreat is named after the great Tibetan sage Gotsangpo, who discovered the Kora circuit of Mount Kailash, is not known. A few smaller caves are found here and the main building is a square white chapel.

Gotsampo Hermitage above Hemis

Chemrey (Druk-pa Kagyu-pa)

Location
47km southeast of Leh, Chemrey is one of the most attractive monasteries, located on top of an impressive hill on the way to Traktok. It is 8km from the road junction at Karu.

How to get there
There is unlikely to be any public transport except in summer. Take a taxi. Don't consider hitching unless you have unlimited time. On the way you pass into a 'poly bag free zone,' a new initiative on the eco front.

Accommodation
None. Basic guesthouses in Karu. Café Jhanta for basic noodles and tea.

About the monastery
The monastery presents a stunning sight. Sitting at the very summit of a steep-sided mountain, it dominates the surrounding fields and valley. Houses and buildings flow down the hill from here to a base cluttered by new and old chortens.

It is the most important branch of Hemis monastery. Begun under Sengge Namgyal and his chief lama Stagsang Raspa, it was probably enlarged as a dedication to Sengge Namgyal after his death. Dates for this are suggested as around 1644–46. It is administered from Hemis and is devoted to the Kagyu-pa sect.

The principle lhakhangs here are the Tsokhang, Lama Lhakhang and Guru Lhakhang, as well as smaller book and butter lamp chambers. An old kitchen may be opened for visitors.

Chemrey Monastery

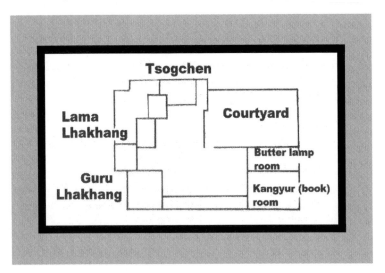

Chemrey Guru Lhakhang displays

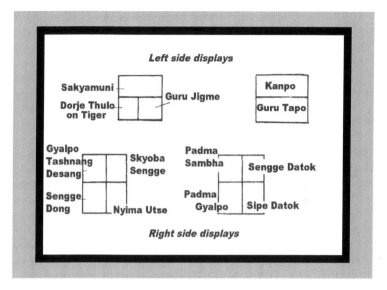

Left side displays

Sakyamuni
Dorje Thulo on Tiger
Guru Jigme

Kanpo
Guru Tapo

Gyalpo Tashnang Desang
Skyoba Sengge
Sengge Dong
Nyima Utse

Padma Sambha
Sengge Datok
Padma Gyalpo
Sipe Datok

Right side displays

Chemrey Guru Lhakhang

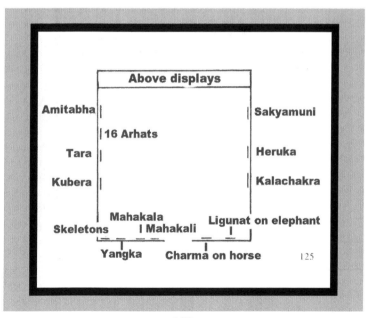

Above displays

Amitabha
16 Arhats
Tara
Kubera
Sakyamuni
Heruka
Kalachakra

Skeletons
Mahakala
Mahakali
Ligunat on elephant
Yangka
Charma on horse

125

103

The Guru Lhakhang is a chamber with a prolific number of deities. It is primarily a chapel dedicated to Guru Rinpoche and many of the images represent differing aspects of the Tantric magician. Set in glass cases on the left are Sakyamuni, Dorje Thulo on a tiger, and Guru Jigme; above are Kanpo and Guru Tapo. To the right, also behind glass, are Gyalpo Tashang Desang, Sokya Sengge, Sengge Dorje and Nyima Utse in one, and Guru Rinpoche, Sengge Datong, Padma Gyalpo and Sipe Datok. The latter might have links to Bon. The great Guru sits overlooking all these accompanying disciples.

On the walls of the Guru Lhakhang one may find Heruka, a wrathful Dhyani Buddha Akshobhya, Mahakala, Amitabha, Tara, Kubera the god of wealth, Kalachakra, Yamantaka and 'Ligi Haton', Chakma on a horse and two amazing skeletons. The sixteen arhats are here to give comfort.

Chemrey Lama Lhakhang

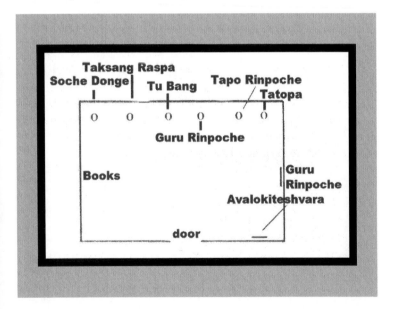

In the Lama Lhakhang, look out for Guru Rinpoche flanked by Soche Donge, Lama Taksang Raspa, the founder of the monastery, Tu Bang, Tapo Rinpoche and Tapopa.

The Tsokhang was unfortunately closed at the time of our visit. This three-storied chapel faces east; there are some prayer wheels here and a courtyard. On the south side is a large book room and next to it a butter lamp chapel.

The main festival here usually falls in November and Cham dances are performed.

Chemrey art

Traktok (Nyingma-pa)

Location
50km southeast of Leh, Traktok clings to a steep hillside on the south side of the valley. To reach it you must first go to Karu, the junction for Hemis, then continue up the valley past Chemrey. Traktok is 15km from Karu. It is a small place and a

tour there is best combined with a visit to other monasteries in this part of the valley.

How to get there
There is unlikely to be any public transport except in summer. Take a taxi. Don't consider hitching unless you have unlimited time. Buses to Tangtse (and Pangong Lake) may pass by in summer.

Accommodation
None.

About the monastery
The monastery clings to a sheer cliff face and has been extended with the addition of a large chamber on the left side. Two large chortens herald your arrival here. The current head lama is Taklung Rinpoche. A small but very attractive monastery, it has an intimate feel to it. Beautiful paintings adorn the walls, both inside the chambers and outside in the courtyard.

Traktok Monastery

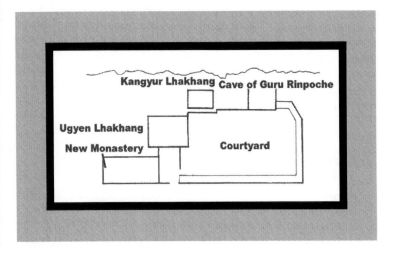

Traktok

The main sanctuary of Traktok (also written as Tak Thog) monastery is one of the meditation caves of Guru Rinpoche (Padma Sambhava). This cave gives the monastery its name, 'natural rock roof cave'. Guarded by yak horns and some imposing guardian deities, the cave shrine is rarely accessible to visitors, since it constitutes the most devotional prayer chamber, often used by a solitary monk in meditation. We and Rama and Joanne were fortunate to visit this holy place, which was dimly lit with a rock floor and rupee notes stuck to the ceiling.

The entrance to the cave up some steep steps has some colourful guardians. On the left is a curious cobra figure, another Lokapala on a horse with his parasol and fruit bowl. Left of the door is Vajrapani (Channa Dorje). On the right are a Mongolian guardian and an unknown image. The cave, known as Tu Phuk, contains an image of Guru Tsang Gyet and eight forms of Guru Rinpoche, as well as an eleven-headed Avalokiteshvara (Chenresig).

Accessed from the platform of the main cave is a chapel to the left; this is the Kangyur Lhakhang. The central Buddha here is flanked by Amitayus on the left, and on the right a four-armed Maitreya and fierce Mahakala, who may be called Tse Phag

107

Med. The right walls exhibit images of Heruka in blue and red forms. A green Mahakala, an unusual sight, is painted on the left wall and another image is called Tsum locally. Images of Heruka dominate the entrance inside walls; one image is a three-headed yab-yum couple.

Traktok Kangyur Lhakhang

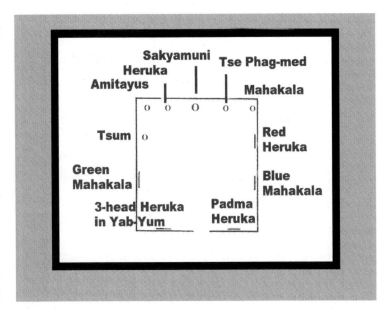

The Urgyen Photang Lhakhang has a number of images devoted to Guru Rinpoche who, as one might expect in a Nyingma-pa monastery, is the prime object of veneration. Sakyamuni is present, as are images of Guru Rinpoche. One has four arms and these are a silver colour. A yab-yum image and a wrathful Guru Rinpoche sit nervously in one corner observing some skeletons. According to the notice board information outside, the images here are called Namsum, Guru Ringzin Thondup, Guru Tak Pho Tsal and Tulkhar.

The large new Lhakhang houses images of Padma Gyalpo, Guru Nang Srith and Zilon in a central position. Also here to the right is Guru Dorje Dolo. The Traktok Tse-Chu **festival** is celebrated on the 9th to 11th days of the 6th month. The Traktok Wangchok festival is conducted from the 26th to 29th days of the 9th month.

Traktok Urgyen Photang Lhakhang

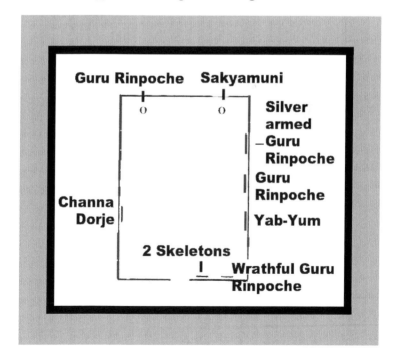

Tangtse

The small settlement at Tangtse is 81km from Karu and about 126km from Leh. There might be some limited public transport in summer, but don't count on it. A small monastery exists here.

Pangong Lake

At a dizzying altitude of 4270m, the long, narrow and strikingly coloured Pangong Lake, which straddles the border between India and China, is 113km from Karu (160km from Leh), and is reached by crossing the Chang La pass, a relatively easy pass except in deep mid-winter. The lake is approximately 130km long and 5–6km wide. Most of it lies in Tibet (China), so it is not possible to do a circuit of the lake. Unfortunately, the Tibetan border is not open here and prospective visitors to that fabled land will just have to dream. Spangmik is the furthest settlement one can visit.

Tso Moriri Lake

The lake lies far to the east and close to the Tibetan border, set within barren rolling landscapes. There is a monastery at Korzok in the Rupshu region where nomadic Changpa herders are found in summer. Despite the harsh climate, marmots, hares and tail-less rabbits scurry about in summer. Brahmini ducks, bar-headed geese, crested grebes and gulls head for the lake in summer.

Chapter Nine

WEST OF LEH

Map of monasteries west of Leh

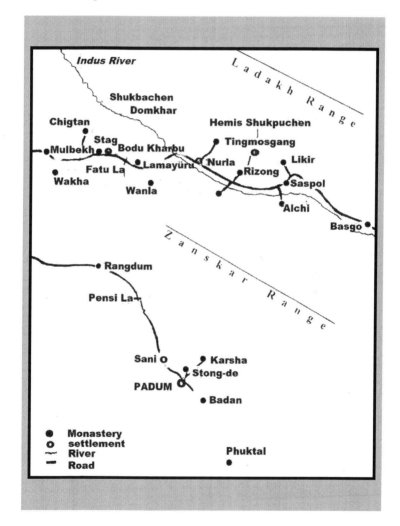

Spituk

Location
Near the end of the airport runway, 7km from Leh.

How to get there
Take a bus towards Lamayuru then get off and walk. It is fairly close to the main road. You could take a taxi from Leh and visit two or three monasteries as part of the same day out.

Accommodation
Stay in Leh.

About the monastery
One of the more famous monasteries of Ladakh, it is one that anyone arriving in Leh by air will gaze at in amazement, as the right wingtip of the plane flying in passes just over it. Standing close to the Indus, the monastery now has road access on the north side. Purists may want to tackle the new stairway from the south, starting close to a large rock with the 'Om Mani Padme Hum' inscription painted on it.

Spituk has close links with Shankar and Stok. It is one of the oldest monasteries in Ladakh, the site being consecrated in the 11th century during the time of Rinchen Zangpo and Yeshe O. It was given its name then as a 'model community', which is what Spituk translates as. Initially a Kadam-pa monastery, it was officially founded by King Gas Ra Bum. Much later in the 15th century, it became a seat of learning for the dominant Gelug-pa. Two emissaries of Tsong Khapa came to Ladakh to grant its full status.

A curious story relates how one of the statues was created from the nose blood of Tsong Khapa, this being the Tsa Phags Med image, which is said to have been hidden in a 3m (10ft) Buddha in the Dukhang at one time. Close links with Tibet in the 15th century made the monastery an important beacon on the western Tibetan plateau. A statue of Jo in the Jokhang (Chokhang) temple was brought from Tibet at that time.

Spituk Monastery

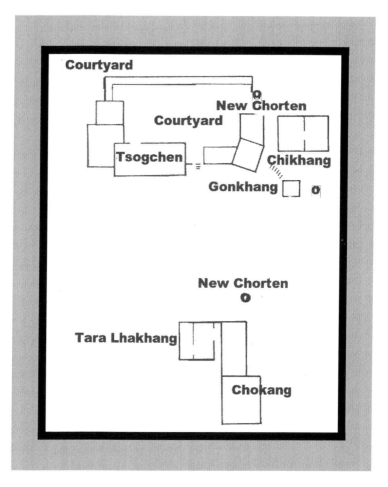

The monastery comprises of a number of welcoming chambers; the main ones are the Chokhang, Tara Lhakhang, Tsogchen, Dukhang-Chikhang, the new golden stupa room on the south side, and the Gonkhang on the hilltop. The large courtyard overlooks the Indus.

Spituk Monastery

The Chokhang is likely to be the first temple visited, for the information board sits close by. A number of thangkas decorate the left wall. A throne for the Rinpoche Kusho Bakula sits here. The other walls bear little decoration, but the main imagery is at the back behind the silver vase and altar lamps. Central is Maitreya, flanked by Guru Rinpoche and Arya Tara, with small images in front. A large silver chorten graces the right and on the left is the Chang Chub chorten on a silver platform. In the extreme corner are a number of robed Buddhas in a chest.

Spituk Chokhang

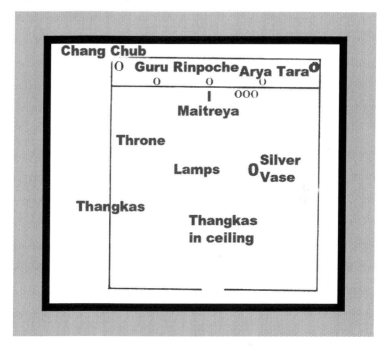

Spituk Tara Lhakhang

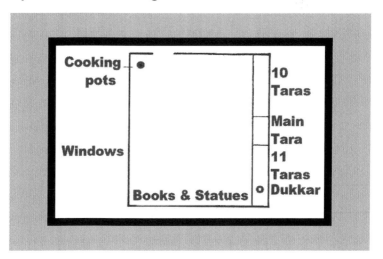

Adjacent to the Chokhang is a slender chamber, in fact two chambers, which house the twenty-one Taras. The Taras reside in an elaborate lacquered display cupboard with four naga - snake supports. The main Tara image is flanked on the left by ten visions with blue sashes. On the right a further eleven sit with silver grey sashes. Also on the right is the female deity with eleven main heads and a thousand arms. A parasol, beads and mace are clear. This image has the name Dukkar Senkar. All the Taras have rainbow-coloured skirts and sit before golden decor, a delightful rhapsody of colour. The adjacent chamber houses many small yellow statues and books.

From the courtyard below, go upstairs into the Tsogchen chapel. Sixteen sturdy wooden pillars hung with golden embroidery support this chamber. Shelves of books line the side walls, and there are also some exquisite paintings. This chamber serves as a prayer room, with five rows of benches for the monks. There are two thrones, one for the Dalai Lama, and butter lamps complete the scene. The back room houses a large 7m-high Sakyamuni, with some large dark statues on the left, and some yellow hat lamas alongside on the right. In the atrium above are many thangkas and fifty-six Buddha figures in all, flanking the earthly Buddha Sakyamuni.

Spituk Tsogchen Lhakhang

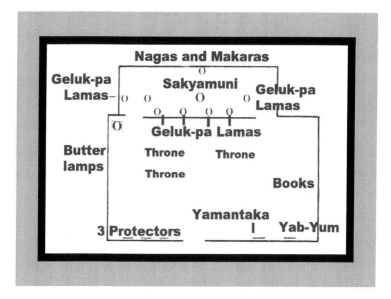

On the west side of the courtyard is a small building housing the memorial stupa built to commemorate the Rinpoche who died some years ago. He is revered as a great man, and was previously a member of parliament and the Indian Ambassador to Mongolia. His reincarnation has recently been found and was enthroned in 2010.

Below the memorial chorten and downstairs to the west again is the Chikhang. It has a small courtyard of its own overlooking the steep crags of the hill with a flagpole centrally located. The Lokapalas welcome in guests.

Inside this chamber are a number of wrathful images, including Yamantaka with seven heads and sixteen arms. Vajra Bhairab, six-armed Mahakala, Palden Lhamo on a horse and Kyitra on a dog can be discerned in here. The first bank of images include a chorten, Sakyamuni Buddha, Avalokiteshvara and a yab-yum. There are two thrones; one for the Dalai Lama and another for the head Rinpoche. In the darker chamber behind one may see two Maitreyas, smaller icons and the head lama's image on the right.

117

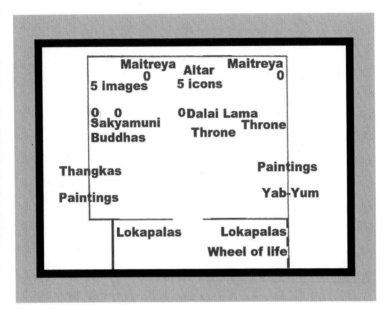

The Gonkhang, or temple of Mahakala, is on the hilltop above the main Spituk complex. The chapel here is dedicated to the protectors and is entered via a small room opening on to the small courtyard. Inside there are some masks, and the main deities are also without exception ferocious and wrathful. Here are both Yamantaka and Mahakala with Pelsay, Gonkha, Namtus, Zinamitra, Kytuba and Nesar. This chapel is around nine hundred years old. All but Yamantaka, whose eyes look out above a scarf, are veiled here.

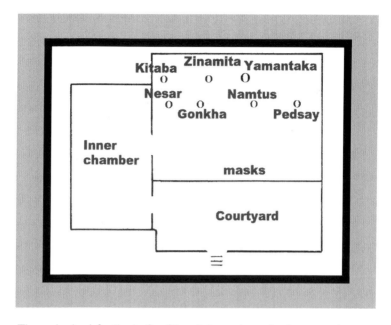

The principal festival, Gu-Stor, takes place in January, i.e. on the 26th to 28th days of the 11th Tibetan month.

Pharka
This minor shrine is across the river close to Spituk and has some caves and a grotto.

Phey
A link road west of Spituk leads to the small settlement of Phey close to the Indus.

Phyang (Drigung Kagyu-pa)

We voted this monastery the most spiritual so far. As we entered we went over to the side and sat on a monk's bench covered with a rug. We sat in meditation, facing a row of monks who were chanting from a text, pages and pages of it. Once in a while some music rang out, a pipe, a large drum, a hand

119

drum, bells and glorious bellowing horns, filling the air with evocative sounds that complimented the chants. Sunlight streamed into the square. I sat enchanted by the scenes.
Joanne Stephenson & Rama Tiwari

Location
About 18km from Leh. The monastery sits up a long gentle slope west of Leh and is surrounded on three sides by the formidable foothills of the Ladakh Range.

How to get there
Take a bus towards Lamayuru. You could take a taxi from Leh and visit two or three monasteries as part of the same day out. By road the monastery is accessed from the rear. Visitors should however also take a road on the south side to visit the extraordinary number of large and small chortens on a hill south of the complex.

Accommodation
Hidden North Guesthouse.

About the monastery
The Phyang Monastery has a charmed location and is one of the oldest such buildings in Ladakh. It is thought to have been founded by Tashi Namgyal in the 16th century. Some historians think he built it out of remorse for the blinding of his elder brother, Lhawang. Probably originally Kadam-pa, this monastery became Drigung-pa nearly five hundred years ago. It is one of two monasteries devoted to this sub-sect of the Kagyu-pa. The Drigung sub-sect has its head monastery in Tibet east of Lhasa. About sixty monks are practising here at present.

Among the chapels here are the Dorje Chang Lhakhang, the Padma Gyalpo chapel, the Tsokhang and the Gonkhang. The three-storied lhakhang on the west side was closed, ostensibly for repair.

Phyang Monastery

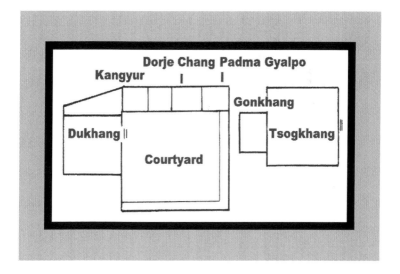

The Dorje Chang Lhakhang (also known as the Dukhang Sarwa) is dedicated to Vajradhara as Dorje Chang. A central altar separates the main images. On the left side are some books and then four deities within a glass cabinet. These are Togden Rinpoche, Kunga Dagspa, Konchok Thinle Zangpo and Dorje Chang. On the right side are an impressive Arya Avalokiteshvara, Skyoba Rinpoche, Sakyamuni and Ratna Shiri. Atisha is seen here as well.

Phyang Dorje Chang Lhakhang

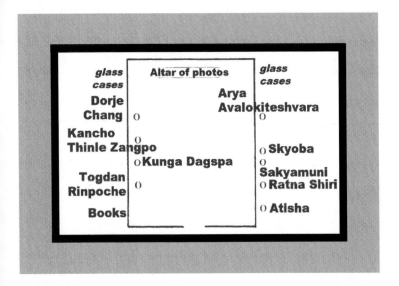

The Padma Gyalpo Lhakhang in the same quadrangle is a smaller chapel dedicated to Padma Gyalpo. There are windows on one side and the doorway is within the wall that is adjacent to the main image. Set behind glass, books and small images in a case flank Padma Gyalpo. On the remaining wall are smallish paintings quite high up.

Padma Gyalpo Lhakhang

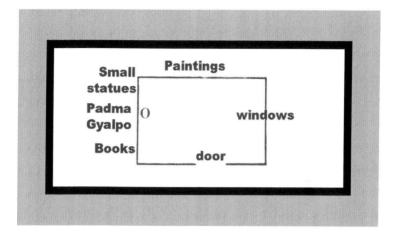

The eastern complex contains two magnificent chambers. The east chapel is the Tsokhang. This amazing room contains a multitude of imagery. Even before entering, one is accosted by the four Lokapalas. On the left hand wall are images of the Dhyani Buddhas and two other lamas, Kunga Takpa and Ratna Shiri, close to the main altar, which is devoted to Skyoba Jigjen. On the right wall are Atisha, Amitabha, Manjushri and Avalokiteshvara, with four arms and his beads. Other little-known characters are Tangla Make, Mutchik Lobdung and some dancing apsara figures.

Tucked away on the west side of the Tsokhang is the Gonkhang. This is a chamber to excite the nerves, for here are the gruesome protectors, those images that one must meditate on to banish bad thoughts. Almost as soon as you enter, a ghastly apparition soars above in the form of a vulture. On the left wall are some paintings of the protectors and a Kalachakra image in a cupboard. On the right are various yab-yum figures; one has two heads and eight arms. The main deity is Mahakala, flanked by Apshi Choskyi Drolma and Garuda. Sing Darma is to the left; all are veiled. Behind this monstrous guard are paintings of Milarepa, Sakyamuni, Dorje Chang and Ratna Shiri.

Phyang Tsokhang

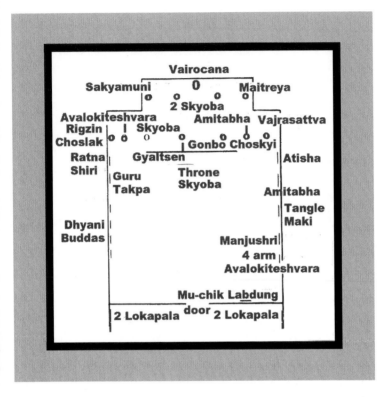

A large thangka is normally unfolded here during the winter festival in February.

Before leaving Phyang, take a stroll along the chorten path, where more than twenty examples, new and old, herald the way to the monastery. From the furthest point you will get an excellent view of the hilltop monastery, the village below and the gleaming white Himalaya behind in the distance.

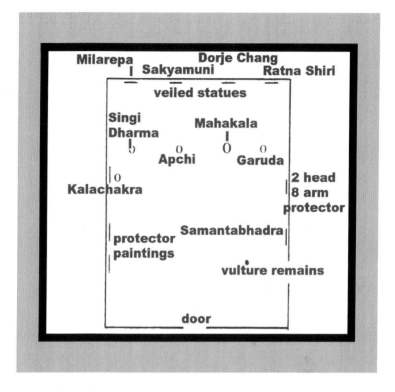

Guru Lhakhang

Also named Lobpon-devi, this small structure is part of Phyang. It is four hundred years old and lies to the north of the main complex. Some of the paintings are similar to those at Alchi. The images here are in a good state of repair and include the Medicine Buddha, a white and an eleven-headed standing Avalokiteshvara. Other deities are a dark blue Hevajra, an eight-armed yab-yum couple, the green Tara, Vajradhara - Dorje Chang, and an image called Ushnisha-vijaya, a painting similar to one at Alchi.

Nimu

35km from Leh, the long sprawling village of Nimu is located at km399 along the main highway, not far after the confluence of the Indus and Zanskar Rivers. A road to the village of Chiling heads south near here. This village is the roadhead for the winter Chaddar treks along the ice-bound Zanskar River, perhaps an apt name as you get off at Chiling for a chilling trek!

The village boasts some very large chortens linked by a long mani wall and the ruins of a castle. There is a large military camp here and a Shiva temple.

Basgo (Kagyu-pa)

Location
About 40km from Leh, on the road to Alchi and Lamayuru.

How to get there
Take a bus towards Lamayuru. You could take a taxi from Leh and visit two or three monasteries as part of the same day out. A link road makes it more accessible; the road is found after the village one km west, and climbs up behind the complex from the north.

Accommodation
None.

About the monastery
Basgo stands like a forlorn couple on a jagged ridge below some rounded mountains. It is in two distinct parts and dominates the small village below. Surprisingly this place was once used by the kings of Ladakh as their capital, perhaps because it had a reliable water supply. The invading Mongols and later the Dogra laid waste to much of the capital. Basgo means bull's head, a link to the protector Yamantaka perhaps?

The fortress that is now in ruins was built under Jamyang and Sengge Namgyal. The upper building houses a large seated three-storey-high image of Maitreya. It is said to have been built under Sengge Namgyal, who brought Nepalese craftsmen from Nepal and established a school at Chiling.

All around are fantastically coloured and executed paintings, on the ceilings as well as the walls. This complex was built by Tsewang Namgyal, the eldest son of the blind King Lhawang in the 16th century. Some Kagyu-pa figures appear on the walls, including Dorje Chang (Vajradhara), Taksang Raspa, Naropa blowing an amazing horn, and Milarepa. Some links to Hindu gods are found here. Vajrapani and possibly Tamdrin are the protectors here.

> A.H. Francke states of Sengge Namgyal and his lama: "*The form of religion of this King and his Lama was that of the red sect... This form of religion has always shown a resemblance to Shaivism (of the Hindu God Shiva).*"

Stag Tsang Raschen (Taksang Raspa), known as the Tiger Lama, was the chief lama associated with Sengge Namgyal and undertook much of the monastic expansion under the king. A mani wall near Basgo is attributed to him, as well as the Leh Palace. Others include Hemis, Chemrey, Tashigang in Tibet, and Hanle well south of Zanskar.

The Serzang Temple has another statue of Maitreya. It is here that one finds the gold and silver decorated Kangyur and Tangyur books. Ser-zang means gold-silver in Tibetan. The small chapel near the Serzang contains a Maitreya, which was dedicated to the wife of Sengge Namgyal, a princess from Baltistan to the north. She was known as Kalzang Drolma, who is linked to goddess Tara (Drolma).

Lower down is the former house of the king's minister, known as the Khalon.

Likir (Gelug-pa)

Location
53km to the west of Leh, up a side valley to the north of the main road to Srinagar, the monastery of Likir stands atop a hill,

with a massive golden statue of Maitreya Buddha behind it, built around 1999.

How to get there
Take a bus towards Lamayuru, get off at the junction and hitch or walk the 5km or so from there. There is unlikely to be much public transport direct to Likir. You could take a taxi from Leh and visit two or three monasteries as part of the same day out.

Accommodation
Norbo Guesthouse
Lotos Guesthouse
Dolkar Guesthouse

About the monastery
The monastery stands majestically on an isolated hill towering above the village and river. Chortens and stupas guard the way up.

Likir is a derivation of the word Klu-Khil, or Kul Naga, which means Snake Coil. It is so-named because the legendary snake king Jokpo slept here, and the hill on which the monastery stands is shaped like a coil. The monastery was founded by sage Lhawang Chosje in 1088, during the reign of King Larchen Gyalpo of Ladakh. He introduced the Kadam-pa teachings, expounded by Atisha. In 1470, during the reign of King Lotos Chokdan, the sage Lhawang Lotos came from Central Tibet and converted this former Kadam-pa monastery to the Gelug-pa sect. The religious rituals and performances are related to Sutra and Tantric ideas.

Inside the monastery many Buddhas, bodhisattvas and deities, scripts and stupas are preserved, symbolising Buddha's body, speech and mind.

Naris Kushok is in charge of the monastery, which has many branches in villages of lower Ladakh. There are one hundred monks practising here.

Likir Monastery

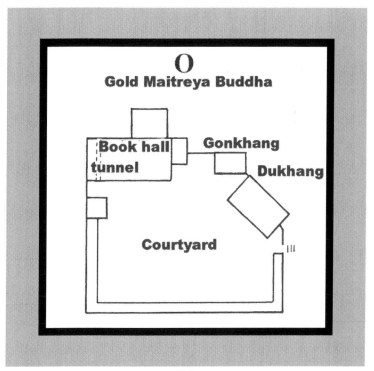

One of the larger chapels is the main Dukhang. The side walls of the Dukhang house the Tibetan religious books, the Kangyur and Tangyur. The main images behind the two thrones include a number of chortens. With strong links to the Dalai Lama, one throne is set aside for his use. Tsong Khapa is much in evidence, as well as the main Sakyamuni Buddha. He is flanked by Dipankar, the first Buddha, known here as Orshung, and on the right is Maitreya. Two large rolled up thangkas are stored in here; one is said to date from the 11th century.

Likir Dukhang

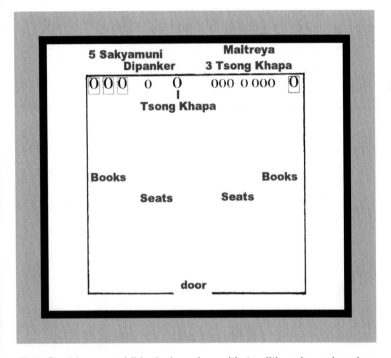

The Gonkhang at Likir, in keeping with tradition, is a chamber for the protectors. Mahakala, Yamantaka and a protector riding a horse are present here. Tsong Khapa and his two disciples sit left of a glass-encased altar. As a rule, women are not allowed into these Gonkhang chambers unless the statues are veiled.

Likir Gonkhang

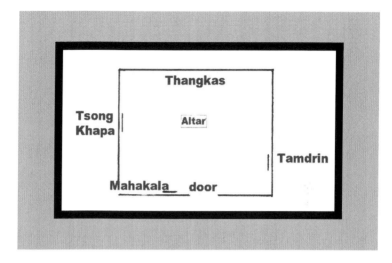

The Lhakhang houses more compilations of the Kangyur and Tangyur as well as an impressive vision of the eleven-headed Avalokiteshvara. The walls are adorned with paintings of the thirty-five benevolent or compassionate Buddhas and Bodhisattvas as well as the sixteen arhats.

Another library and book hall is located above the tunnel that leads to the massive imposing Buddha behind the complex to the north. Another chapel, which was closed at the time of our visit, houses Tsong Khapa, Sakyamuni and an altar to Thugje Chenpo, according to local monks.

The 25m-high golden image of Maitreya behind the monastery stands imposingly facing east.

Saspol

Saspol is an open, merry place. Around it are many monasteries. At the very road is a small monastery, and within it a gigantic image of the seated Maitreya. On the side also stand giants, Manjushri and Avalokiteshvara. In the font temple is an ancient stone stela with the same images, which dates from the 10th century or earlier. The lama of the temple talks with knowledge about Maitreya. This temple has been little noticed in descriptions.
Altai Himalaya: *Nicholas Roerich 1929*

The spread-out village of Saspol is a small regional centre, being close to Likir, Alchi and Rizong. Dominating the northern skyline is a crumbling fort with some meditation caves close by. On a hill to the northeast is a new-looking chapel. Just off the main street to the north is the village monastery, the Chamba Gompa. Saspol is 373km from Srinagar and 61km from Leh. A cluster of chortens can be viewed about 2km east of the village.

Alchi (Kagyu-pa Gelug-pa)

Location
About 66km from Leh, just south of Saspol.

How to get there
Take a bus towards Lamayuru, get off at the junction and hitch or walk from there. There may be a direct bus to Alchi in season. You could take a taxi from Leh and visit two or three monasteries as part of the same day out. Close to Alchi, the Zanskar Range has jagged formations and almost intoxicating rock strata designs. Chortens and mani walls welcome the visitor expectant with anticipation.

Accommodation
Alchi Resort, an expensive but pleasant place
Samdubling Guesthouse
Potala Guesthouse
Zimskhan Holiday Hotel off the entrance path to Alchi complex
Lungpa Guesthouse near the main complex

About the monastery

From the main parking area a path leads east towards the river to Alchi's main compound. On the way a sign informs you that an original walking stick of Rinchen Zangpo is seen on the right. Quite where, though, remains a mystery. According to legend, it has grown into the tree that stands nearby. There are some chortens before the main gateway.

Alchi is one of the oldest monasteries in the region, dating from the 11th century. Said to have been founded by Kalden Shesrab, it was built under Rinchen Zangpo and his Kashmiri artists. Its paintings show the distinct Kashmiri/Indian style. On flat terrain, it consists of a maze of courtyards and corridors. There are a number of chapels here, including the Manjushri Lhakhang, Lotsa (Lotsawa) Lhakhang, Sum Tsek Lhakhang, Kangyur Lhakhang and the Lhakhang Soma, as well as some significant chortens. Alchi used to have high walls known as *cags-ri* around the Chos complex, similar to the walls at Tabo in Spiti. The wooden arch over the Sum Tsek is an example of a trifoliate arch, a decorative wooden feature.

Alchi interior art

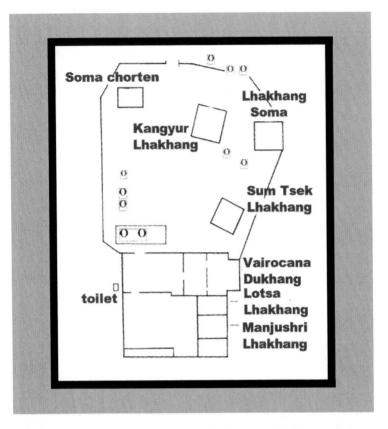

Originally of the Kagyu-pa sect, it is now administered from Likir under the Gelug-pa. We will begin our description at the far end of the complex, in the Manjushri chapel. Alchi never fails to impress, for here are four elaborate, colourful and stunning images. A dazzling golden vision of Manjushri welcomes visitors. Flanked, as are all four images, by strange-looking elephants, snow lions, bird figures and a cupid-like top image, the impression is one of overload. These figures are reminiscent of the 'four harmonious brothers'. Moving around clockwise, the next image is the white Manjushri, followed by the red and then the blue version. All are surrounded by the curious animal figures and each holds a khata scarf. Beside the entry door on the wall are Tsong Khapa, Avalokiteshvara

(Chenresig), Sakyamuni, Tara and two newer protectors lower down, probably Vajrapani and Hayagriva.

Alchi Manjushri Lhakhang

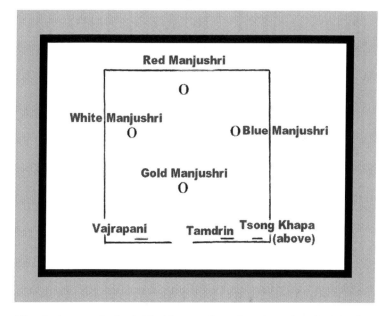

The Lotsawa (Lotsa) Lhakhang, the chamber devoted to the translator (Lotsawa), is dedicated to Rinchen Zangpo. His painted image sits to the left of the central Sakyamuni, facing towards the Buddha. A thin white Avalokiteshvara, offering compassion and holding his rosary beads, appears on the right of the Buddha. Mandalas on the remaining walls are surrounded by thousands of Buddha and Bodhisattva images. On the west side is a red image of Amitayus, and Akshobhya is on the east wall. A blue Mahakala poses over the doorway inside.

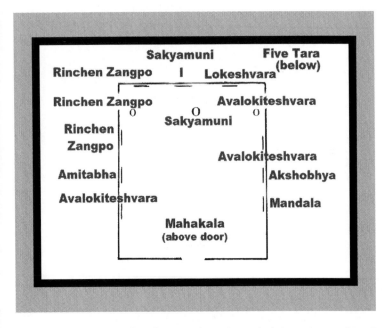

Continuing west, the large chapel and internal courtyard structure is the main temple, the Dukhang or Vairocana Lhakhang. There are two main lhakhangs in here; the smaller one on the right is devoted to Maitreya. The larger chamber is devoted to Vairocana, the fifth and usually unseen Dhyani Buddha.

Within the open area are a number of intricate wall paintings. On the right is a new mandala decorated in many colours and constructed of sand grains. To the right behind this is the chamber containing a large four-armed, standing statue of Maitreya. Paintings of Guru Rinpoche, the Medicine Buddha and Milarepa watch him from the left wall. Tsong Khapa and Tara observe from the right wall.

Before entering the main shrine there are further deities to observe. On the left is Avalokiteshvara and a three-headed protector (Tamdrin?) in yab-yum. One image is said to be

Tsepe Pakmit. On the right are three standing Buddhas, the Trushok Buddhas.

Alchi (Vairocana) Dukhang

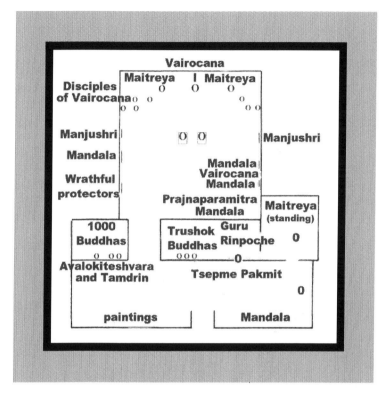

Once into the main chapel of Vairocana, two chortens form the central area and behind these is the central dominant image of Vairocana flanked by smaller aspects of the same deity. The main image has two south-facing heads and at least two others on the side. Above sit snake-like protectors.

The superb mandalas on the walls around the chamber depict Vairocana (four-faced white), a green Tara and the four Dhyani Buddhas in wrathful mode on the left, and Manjushri to the right. Further along the left side wall are more mandalas with different aspects of Manjushri, and then a thousand Buddhas are displayed close to the main statues. Near the doorway to its right (on entry) is a circular, slightly damaged mandala with Prajnaparamita, goddess of wisdom, at its centre. These mandalas are up to 3m (10ft) across. Above the door again is Mahakala.

Exiting the courtyard and passing under the large chortens on your left, you reach an ancient-looking three-storied building with an elaborate beautifully carved wooden façade. This is the Sum Tsek temple, and it is covered with exquisite murals and paintings. Inside are three enormous bodhisattvas set around a central stupa. Heading clockwise, look out for the green Tara on the wall, just before the first massive standing image. This is Avalokiteshvara, offering great compassion. In the next recess is the red Maitreya, of equal height and standing. The third recess houses Manjushri, again standing at equal height. He is a creamy colour. All three have elaborately designed, gaily decorated legs. Just before coming to the Manjushri statue there is a magnificent yellow painted image of Manjushri on the wall. Depictions of Amitabha and Akshobhya are in abundance here, and many walls have thousands of Buddha images. Horse paintings dominate some of the ceiling.

The upper levels display yet more magnificent imagery. Here the Dhyani Buddhas and their female accomplices are much in evidence in mandala form. Avalokiteshvara appears in red, white and blue colours and here also is the dominant deity Vairocana in differing aspects. Access to this level may be difficult.

Alchi Sum Tsek Lhakhang

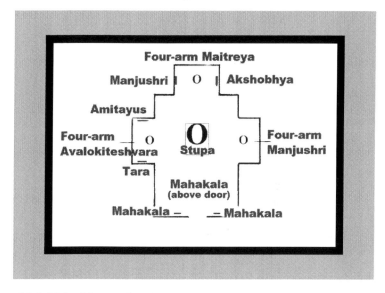

Alchi Lhakhang Soma

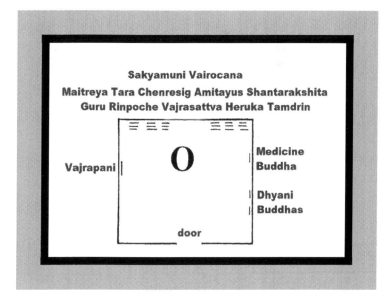

The Kangyur Lhakhang is the next building on the right here. It houses the books of the Tibetan bibles, the Kangyur and Tangyur. It was closed.

Behind this building, and easily missed by some guides, is one more chapel, the Lhakhang Soma. It is a smallish structure but its artistry cannot be dismissed. The paintings here have a more Kashmiri look about them. Many are outstanding. There are a lot of images of the protectors. On the left wall are a number of mandalas set within Buddha images. Vajrapani is one protector here. On the right are images of the Medicine Buddha holding his bowl and the Dhyani Buddhas. The back wall has an array of Buddhist talent; many are wrathful. Look here for Vajrapani, Guhya Manjuvara in yab-yum, and Kalachakra also embracing his consort. Central is Vairocana, wearing a red gown and surrounded by his disciples. On the right are more guardians, different aspects of Heruka with his consort, as well as Tamdrin.

As you turn to leave, look for the famous scenes from the life of the Buddha on your right. A strange-looking Mahakala bids you farewell above the doorway.

Other Buddhist shrines in the vicinity include the place called Shang Rong dedicated to Guru Rinpoche. It belongs to the Druk-pa branch of the Kagyu-pa. The Satapuri Monastery, sometimes known as the Dugyaling, has a number of chapels. It was closed, unfortunately.

Alchrikh

Alchrikh is a little-known and rarely visited settlement well south of the main highway east of Alchi. It is noted for an ancient Mahakala image.

Hemis Shukpuchan

Not to be confused with the important monastery of Hemis southeast of Leh, this small village on the Likir to Tingmosgang trek is a noted stopover where guests may stay with local people.

Uletokpo

This pleasant spot overlooking the Indus is awash with colour in spring. Nearby is the village of Lardo, which is famed for its apricots in season. There are a few camping places at Uletokpo, which is a convenient base for exploring Rizong.

Rizong (Gelug-pa)

Location
70km west of Leh, 5km north of the road to Lamayuru and Srinagar.

How to get there
Either take a taxi from Leh for the day, or take a bus to Lamayuru and get off. Only do this if you are prepared to take your chances on finding accommodation at the monastery; there is no village here. Rizong is reached by a small track which is often cut off by snow in winter, as indeed it was during our visit. It is a long walk from the main road; don't believe the sign that says 2km – that is the distance to the nunnery. After the nunnery you will soon reach an unmarked junction near some stupas. Take the left fork, which is also a jeep track, and follow this uphill. The road straight on goes eventually to Yangtang, but also forks and doubles back further on to Rizong, if you prefer a less steep path. The walk to Rizong from the main road will take about 1hr 20mins, depending on your state of acclimatisation.

Accommodation
None. Try Uletokpo, or continue to Lamayuru.

About the monastery
Rizong is one of the more unusual monasteries in Ladakh. Before reaching the main complex you pass the nunnery. This is called Chullichan and is about 2.5km from the main road, set in a small grove of trees. The valley offers little sunshine, making it bitterly cold in winter. It is a simple building with a courtyard and suffers from little sunlight.

Rizong (also Ri Dzong) monastery, further up the hill, is well hidden and only displays its imposing presence at the last minute. The monastery sits high on a steep-sided hillside but, unlike many others, it does not command an all-round vista. A new arched entrance and chorten greet the visitor. Beyond, below the main complex, are the new monks' quarters. A path leads steeply up into a maze of buildings, through to the upper chapels and courtyards. There is no village here, so the monastery stands in isolation. The monastery is of no great antiquity, having been founded around 1840. It was built under the supervision of Lama Tsultrin Nyima. It conforms to the reformist sect, the yellow hats, and the monk population is reportedly more than forty.

Rizong Monastery

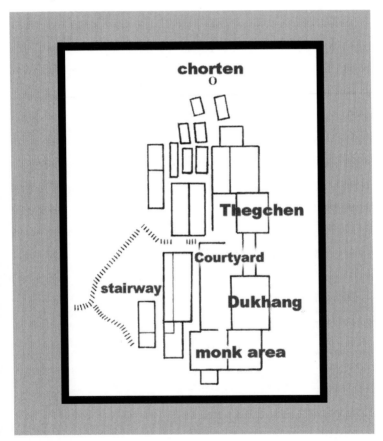

There are two main chapels that visitors can view. The Dukhang, on the right, houses two chortens dedicated to Se Rinpoche and Tsultrin Nyima. Elephants, lions and human figures flank the main chorten. The Sakyamuni Buddha here is wearing a crown and not his more familiar hair. Maitreya is prominent to the right, and in front of the Se Rinpoche chorten are eight small images of Buddha and a Guru Rinpoche. Avalokiteshvara and Rinchen Buddha are on the left of the main chortens. The paintings on the walls are relatively recent and feature various scenes from the Buddha's life. On the left is a painting of the oddly named Dru pal and Avalokiteshvara (Chenresig). Above near the door is a large rolled up thangka held up in the roof.

Rizong Monastery

Rizong Thegchen Lhakhang

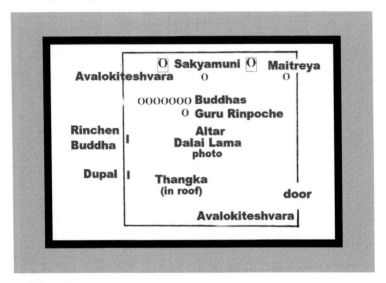

Rizong Dukhang

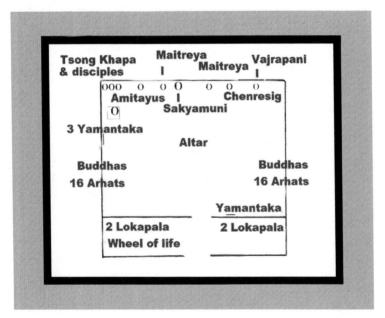

The other chapel here is the Thegchen, the yellow-coloured building that tops the complex. This chamber is probably the more interesting of the two; it houses some imposing images. The main icons are behind the throne and altar. Sakyamuni takes centre stage, flanked by Maitreya on each side. To the right are a fine Avalokiteshvara and a fearsome Vajrapani. On the left are Amitayus and Tsong Khapa. Buddhas and Arhats grace the side walls, and a vision of Yamantaka protects the inside entry wall on the right. Outside are the familiar Lokapalas, the wheel of life and two images said to be of Chakra (Chakra Sambhava?) and (Palden?) Lhamo.

Mangyu

Almost south of Uletokpo along a new link road is the village of Mangyu. It is said to date back to the 11th century and may well have had links to Rinchen Zangpo. An eroded chorten dates from that time. The four chapels are devoted to Maitreya, Chenresig, Dorje Sempa Khang (also known as Dorje Cenpo) and Vairocana. Vairocana is accompanied by the other Dhyani Buddhas. The chapels here are now looked after by Nyingma-pa monks.

Tingmosgang (Gelug-pa Druk-pa)

Location
Tingmosgang (Tingmogang) is north of the main Leh–Kargil highway and is the concluding point for those who trek here from Likir, a three to four-day trip.

How to get there
Take any Kargil-bound bus and hop off approximately 11km after Uletokpo. A taxi will cost close to Rs3000 return.

Accommodation
Try local houses.

About the monastery
Built on top of a rocky spur, its location is one of the main attractions of this ancient fort, monastery and village. Despite

the ravages of war and time, there is much to be enjoyed here. Many of the remains still exhibit excellent artwork.

The earliest mention of Tingmosgang is in chronicles about King Grags Bum lde, who is said to have been advised by Tsong Khapa to build four Chang Chub stupas set in the four directions. He was also directed to add a statue of Maitreya as well. There is fleeting evidence that the Dards also occupied the place. Later, when defending the country against the Mongols, the Ladakhis held out at Basgo and Tingmosgang. They were only relieved by the intervention of the Kashmiri forces.

A nunnery was established in 1996 under Dutch patronage, in association with the Buddhist Committee of Ladakh.

An 8m-tall Maitreya resides in the two-storied red chapel, together with some Tara figures and one of the Bodhisattva of longevity – Vijaye.

One may observe here a good example of the three chortens together representing Manjushri, Avalokiteshvara (Chenresig) and Vajrapani (Channa Dorje). The icons are displayed behind the chortens. A similar example can be seen just south of Shankar in Leh.

The Guru Rinpoche Lhakhang is around four hundred years old. The shrine houses the Tantric magician Guru Rinpoche and his two consorts, Yeshe Tsogyal and Mandavara.

The chapel devoted to Chenresig is said to house an image of Avalokiteshvara, but in this case the image is probably a Lokeshvara, of which there are 108 differing aspects. It might well be confusing. The Lokeshvara images and deities are found more commonly in Nepal.

Lamayuru (Drigung – Kagyu-pa)

Whoever built Lamayuru and Mulbekh knew what was true beauty and fearlessness. Before such expanse, before such decorations, Italian cities pale. And these solemn rows of stupas are like joyous torches upon tourmaline sands... Where lies a country equal to these forsaken spots? Let us be just and bow before such true beauty.
Altai Himalaya: *Nicholas Roerich*

Location
Approximately 125km from Leh along the main highway to Kargil and Srinagar.

How to get there
Buses run regularly in summer but in winter services are limited, often alternate days. It takes up to six hours by bus. A taxi will take three hours and cost around Rs3000 for the return trip. It will be a rush though in one day.

Accommodation
Monastery Guesthouse, the Niranjana
Local Guesthouses, Shangri-La and Dragon.

About the monastery
The monastery and village have one of the most spectacular settings of any in Ladakh. Hemmed in by strangely eroded spires and organ pipe features, the scene presents an alluring vision of a mediaeval lost world above the Drogpo River. It was once called the Yungdrung monastery, which means its origins lie with the Bon faith of early Tibet. This makes it one of the oldest monasteries in Ladakh. It also had the name Tharpa Ling, which means 'place of freedom', because miscreants could seek refuge in the monastery.

According to one legend, the area once lay under a lake full of Naga spirits. A learned teacher, the Arhat Nyimagung, is said to have dried up this lake and made the land fit for a shrine. Lamayuru is now one of two major Drigung Kagyu-pa gompas in Ladakh. The Drigung was founded by Skyoba Jigjen Gonpo in 1179, northeast of Lhasa at Drigung Til in the Kyichu river valley. However they did not formally possess the monastery from the Kadam-pa until the 16th century. Around two hundred monks study here.

Lamayuru Monastery

Large stupas and chortens are clustered near the main structure, which houses the Dukhang, Chenresig Lhakhang and the Gonkhang. Well below the main structure is the older section of the Sengge Lhakhang.

The oldest part of the monastery dates back to the 11th century, to the time of Rinchen Zangpo. It is called the Sengge Lhakhang and is all that remains of possibly five lhakhangs from that time. The main image, as was common in the 11th century, is that of Vairocana, the fifth Dhyani Buddha set on a Garuda figure. On each side are the four other Dhyani Buddhas, Amitabha, Amoghasiddhi, Akshobhya and Ratna Sambhava, with frescoes of mandalas, Vairocana, and wrathful deities on the walls. Attached to this chamber is the old Gonkhang. The wrathful deities here are Yamantaka, Hayagriva (Tamdrin, also called Bek-Tse in Ladakh) and Mahakala.

148

Lamayuru Sengge Lhakhang

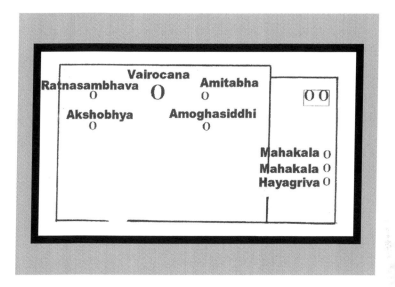

Lamayuru Chenresig Lhakhang

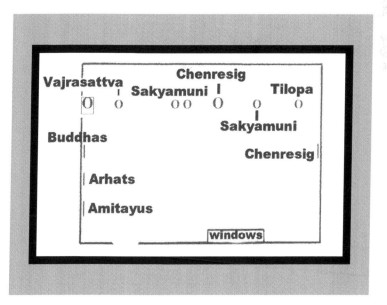

The Chenresig Lhakhang is devoted to Avalokiteshvara, depicted in his eleven-headed thousand-armed version. Sakyamuni and Tilopa, the Indian master, are on the left and on the right are Vajrasattva and Sakyamuni. Various Buddhas and mandalas paintings adorn the walls.

The main dukhang is a newer chapel. The four Lokapalas and a Wheel of Life grace the entrance veranda to the Dukhang. Inside and to the right is the meditation cave of Naropa and Marpa, the principle founder of the Kagyu-pa. His famed disciple Milarepa is found here in the cave. The main image here is of Skyoba Jigjen, the founder of the Drigung sect, with a large hat. Other deities here are Sakyamuni, Guru Rinpoche, Nangsten, Thinle Zangpo and Dontup Chopsgyal. An inner shrine houses Tara.

Lamayuru New Dukhang

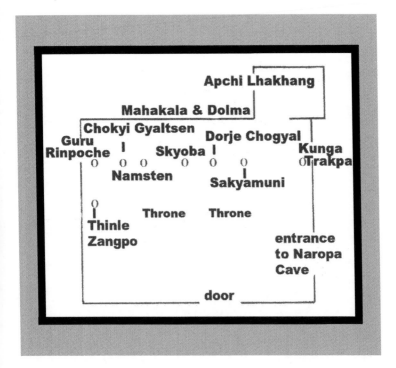

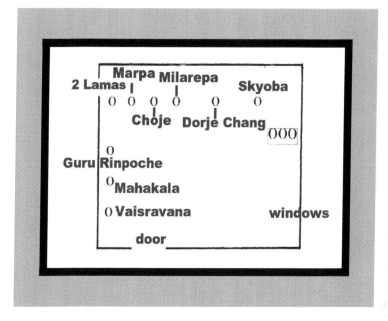

The gonkhang is located above the dukhang and houses some more common deities. Here we find Skyoba Jigten, Dorje Chang, Milarepa, Marpa, Guru Rinpoche, Lama Cho-Je, plus a four-armed Mahakala and Vaisravana, the protectors.

Another chapel, often closed, is the Rangdol Nyima Lhakhang.

Atiche

This isolated monastery south of Lamayuru belongs to the Drigung Kagyu-pa order and has to be accessed on foot. The main images, in statue form, are Dorje Chang, Rinchen Zangpo and Dontup Chogyal.

Wanla

This dramatically located edifice high on an unassailable ridge lies to the south of Lamayuru and can only be accessed currently by walking. The narrow river gorges around here wind in and out of the mountains and one might sometimes need to ford the rivers. This complex has links to Rinchen Zangpo. A statue of Avalokiteshvara (Chenresig) is a significant deity here.

Kanji

Kanji is a small village southwest of Lamayuru, located at the base of the pass, the Kanji La, which links Rangdum in Zanskar to Lamayuru. A small village gompa is found here, of interest to those on trek.

Bod Kharbu

This is a small settlement and has a monastery overlooking the Indus River. It is mentioned in chronicles of Ladakh, but it is chiefly noted for its location as a significant settlement of the Purig region. Like Chigtan, it was embroiled in the 16th century power struggles.

Moorcroft, the early English visitor, commented on its rich fertile fields. "*It was the finest crop I ever beheld; and a spirited English farmer would have thought himself sufficiently repaid for a ride of many miles by a sight of it.*"

The lama's residence at Bod Kharbu is a nearly windowless three-storey mud brick building.

Stag and Mudig

These two isolated places are about half way between Mulbekh and Lamayuru. Of the two, Stag is the more impressive, although little remains. It is the setting and location of Stag fortress and village that is dramatic. Mudig is a small chapel close by.

Chigtan

Formally an important crossroads of Muslim and Buddhist culture, the ruins of Chigtan lie around 10km north of the main highway east of Mulbekh. Chigtan lies in the heart of the region known as Purig.

Chigtan had long vacillated between being Buddhist or Muslim. It was ambivalent for some time about Islam, after its partial conversion in the late 16th century. A quarrel between the Chigtan Sultan and his neighbour at Kalatse ensured interference from Jamyang Namgyal, the Ladakhi King. Despite this, the Baltis under Ali Mir took control and were not repelled until Deldan Namgyal arrived in around 1673.

Towering above are the ruins of an impressive fort. It rises in a series of mud-walled levels to a dramatic upper citadel. A few wooden pillars remain here. Another ruin sits on the adjacent hill.

A monastery here dates back to the 11th century and Rinchen Zangpo. It closed at the end of the 19th century. When A. H. Francke visited, only two Muslim guardians were looking after it and he ascertained that some Buddhist Dards occasionally came to pray there.

Mulbekh

In ancient Mulbekh, a gigantic image of the Coming One powerfully stands beside the road. Every traveller must pass by this rock. Two hands reach toward the sky, like the summons of far-off worlds. Two hands reach downward like the benediction of earth. They know that Maitreya is coming.
Altai Himalaya: *Nicholas Roerich*

Location
190km west of Leh on the main road to Srinagar, 45km before Kargil.

How to get there
Get the bus from Leh to Srinagar or Lamayuru, and get off on the way. Mulbekh is on the main road.

Accommodation
J&K Tourist Bungalow.

About the shrine
For those coming from Muslim-dominated Kargil and Srinagar (if safe), Mulbekh will be almost the first encounter with the Buddhist culture. It is where Muslim Kashmir merges with Buddhist Ladakh. The area was formerly known as Purig. It has long been a crossroads for travellers and merchants.

In a dramatic setting, carved into an enormous rocky outcrop, stands an 8m-high four-armed Buddha figure of Maitreya, called Chamba by the Tibetans and local people. On his head stands a stupa. This statue was carved into a single boulder during the 5–6th centuries, in what is known as the 'Kushana' style, a style more associated with Ghandara. There are two gompas here: Serdung, which is Druk-pa and is responsible to Chemrey, and Gandentse, which is Gelug-pa and comes under the supervision of Likir. To reach Gandentse entails an arduous uphill walk, so not many visitors make it that far. The ruined former palace of the Chalon Rajas remains to the north.

Wakha

South of Mulbekh on the opposite bank of the river, the Wakha complex and village sit at the base of a high, craggy outcrop. The small monastery is set precariously above and houses a shrine of Avalokiteshvara.

Shergol

Shergol, 236km from Srinagar, is a couple of kilometres off the main road, between Kargil and Mulbekh in the Wakha valley. It is a hard ascent to this monastery, built on a bluff. Following the Gelug-pa sect, it has a small shrine with an eleven-headed Avalokiteshvara image, and three wooden Tibetan Tara images. The views are more impressive than the art inside, which is sadly faded and dusty. The word 'gompa' means solitary retreat, and nowhere is this more apt a description. The mythical founder is Agu Drumba.

Gyal

No one need visit Gyal to see paintings or images. Rather there is an atmosphere of deep peace in which it might be possible to approach an intuitive understanding of what it is that the lamas, and all men, are seeking... here, if anywhere, a man might come close to the heart of things...
Ladakh: Crossroads of High Asia: *Janet Rizvi*

This tiny remote gompa, high up the Wakha valley, will probably not be visited by any readers of this book, but we feel this quote encapsulates the feeling one might hope to achieve during a visit to Ladakh.

Kargil

Location
About 234km from Leh and 204km from Srinagar.

How to get there
Get the bus from Leh to Srinagar. Kargil is the halfway point and overnight stop. It is also not recommended at present at it is the base for the Indian Army operations on the Line of Control between India and Pakistan.

Accommodation
Hotel Greenland has been going for many years, although that doesn't make it any more of a choice.
J&K Tourist Bungalow
Caravan Serai
Hotel Siachen

About the town
Kargil is firmly set in the Muslim zone of Ladakh, with mainly Shia faithful. Before partition it was on the trade route to Skardu and Baltistan. Buses from Srinagar to Leh halt here overnight.

Chapter Ten

NORTH OF LEH

North of Leh, the road to the Khardung La Pass claims to be the highest motorable road in the world, though there must now be some other contenders for this title in Tibet and perhaps Bolivia. From the Khardung La, the road drops down into the fertile Nubra valley, where apricots and other delicacies flourish in the summer months. But in the bleak winters, when temperatures drop sometimes way below -40°C and the road is cut off for many months, life goes into hibernation.

The monasteries are described in outline only, since only devoted scholars or those with a keen interest in Buddhist monasteries will take the time to travel to these more distant places.

Nubra Valley

Diskit (Gelug-pa)

> *Right behind the village the mountainside is cleft by a wild, extremely narrow, deep gorge with perpendicular walls... At the top, upon a marked spur of this ridge, is perched the ancient Gompa of Deskit, hanging right over the village and the oasis...*
> **Giotto Dainelli: Buddhists and Glaciers of Western Tibet**

Location
150km or so from Leh, this is an important branch of Thikse.

How to get there
Enquire about a travel permit a couple of days in advance. Private car is the only way to go. The road leads up and over the spectacular Khardung La.

Accommodation
There are four or five guesthouses here open in summer. Spangla has been recommended.

About the monastery
Established in the early 15th century, it was founded by Shenrap Zangpo and had links to Stakna and Karsha. The monastery sits on a very steep, rugged crag overlooking the village; the steps up to it are some of the steepest in Ladakh! The temple is filled with wrathful guardians and deities to protect the dharma from evil spirits. Most of them are covered in fine materials. Another place of worship has a brass lock encrusted with precious stones. Inside there's a long, beautiful hall with wooden floors and posts draped with long colourful flags. A Buddha sits behind glass and a huge decorative drum adorns the room. Up yet more steps is another small chapel, with plain red pillars and various seated Buddhas housed in glass cases with red decorative frames.

Chambra

Location
In Hunder, a village about 6km from Diskit. This is the place to see Bactrian two-humped camels wandering in the sands.

About the monastery
A small gompa and chortens overlook the river and desert. The gompa is rust-red in colour with a concrete path leading to the front. There's a small anteroom before the main temple. A large Buddha sits behind glass; the skylight above makes the whole atmosphere luminescent. A small 1000-handed statue of Avalokiteshvara sits to one side. On the other side is a bookcase full of elaborately covered books. Faded frescoes adorn the walls.

Samtenling

Location
Above the village of Sumur.

How to get there
After leaving Diskit heading east, turn north along the Nubra River.

About the monastery
Again, it has many decorative red columns and pillars supporting a balcony and ceilings. Up another set of stairs from the main gompa is a small chapel, with Maitreya on the left, a metallic chorten in the middle and another Buddha on the right. The walls are covered with murals of seated Buddhas. Not yet two hundred years old, it is a lively place with many young monks studying there.

Panamik

Famous for its hot springs, local people come from far and wide to bathe in its therapeutic waters to cure many ailments. There is a small guesthouse attached to the hot springs. At least two hours walk from here is the Ensa monastery, a relatively recent structure.

Chaddar River in winter

Chapter Eleven

ZANSKAR

These monasteries and villages are described in outline only, since only devoted scholars and those with a keen interest in Buddhist monasteries will take the time to travel to these more distant places. However, passing trekkers may also find something of interest to divert their attention from their tired feet or frozen extremities!

Chiling

About 19km up the Zanskar River from Nimu is the village of Chiling, where the winter Chaddar trek, walking up the frozen ice of the Zanskar river, starts and ends. Here is a community of Nepalese artisans, whose ancestors were brought from Nepal to make the giant Buddha statues at Shey. Nowadays they work in silver, copper and brass, making everyday utensils as well as those for religious use. See Bibliography for the lost wax method.

Rangdum (Gelug-pa)

Set in the wide Suru valley at around 3600m on an outcrop surrounded by stony river plains, Rangdum monastery is a simple structure. To the north across the Kanji La pass is an ancient trade route to Lamayuru. The monastery belongs to the Gelug-pa sect and at times up to 50 monks live here. The main images are Tsong Khapa, Sakyamuni and Chenresig.

Zangla

About 5km from Padum, Zangla is the starting point for many treks, including the winter trek known as the Chaddar trek, when trekkers who are not already too cold walk along the frozen river Zanskar towards Nimu. The ruins of Zangla castle sit on a hill overlooking the town, and an old **nunnery** still functions nearby.

Tsa-zar

Halfway between Zangla and Stongde, the frescoes in this monastery are worth a visit.

Stongde (Gelug-pa)

18km north of Padum, this is a beautiful old monastery associated with Marpa. The village below is like an oasis in the desert. Stongde is the second largest monastery in Zanskar, housing around sixty monks. The gonkhang, home to many impressively fierce deities, is the most eye-catching of several temples here. It's a hard climb to get here, but worth the effort if you can make it.

Karsha (Gelug-pa)

Roughly 9km from Padum, Karsha, the main monastery of Zanskar, makes an imposing spectacle and can be seen from far away. Gelug-pa is the sect of this monastery. As with Rangdum, it comes under the patronage of Tensing Chogyal, a brother of the Dalai Lama. It has four chapels containing various statues and other artworks, including some beautiful silver and copper chortens. The Lhabrang temple is particularly interesting. The main deities here are Sakyamuni, Chenresig, Maitreya and Tsong Khapa.

Nearby is a nunnery called **Dorje Dzong**; the ruins here are thought to be the original foundations of the monastery. Here is also an old stupa with original murals, and the ancient temple of **Chukshik-jal**, with some fine frescoes damaged by smoke.

Sani (Druk-pa Kagyu-pa)

Some 8km from Padum, in the Suru valley, is the castle-like monastery of Sani. Unlike most others, it sits on the valley floor, and is noted for its chortens and mani walls. It belongs to the Druk-pa Kagyu-pa sect. To the rear of the monastery is the Kanika Stupa, indicating a connection with Kanishka, the Kushan ruler of the 2nd century. The main chapel contains various statues of deities, and the walls are covered with frescoes and thangkas. A smaller neglected chapel at the back contains even more interesting paintings, depicting the life of Padma Sambhava/Guru Rinpoche. Some remains of the Indian master, Naropa, are reputedly buried here.

Outside the monastery is an old cemetery surrounded by ancient Indian art in the form of rock carvings.

Padum

This is the main settlement of the Zanskar valley, with a population of almost 2500. Nearly half the inhabitants are Muslim. The old town consists of adobe houses and chortens, and a hill on which used to stand the old palace and fort. New buildings and an extended market are spreading along the road. Padum is famous as the main trekking base, and with road access is now also a tourist destination for other visitors.

There is a large boulder showing 8th-century Buddhist rock carvings near the bank of the Lungnak river. About one hour's walk above the town, on a relatively easy path, is the small monastery of **Stagrimo**, said to house thirty lamas. On the other side of the valley an interesting-looking monastery clings to a hilltop; this is **Pibiting**, built in the shape of a stupa.

Bardan (Druk-pa Kagyu-pa)

12km south of Padum, this is believed to have been founded in the 17th century as the first Kagyu-pa monastery in Zanskar. It controls Sani monastery, as well as other smaller ones in the area, and houses around forty lamas. Another crag-top edifice, it is on the trekking route to Manali. Inside the main hall are some beautiful statues and stupas.

Phuktal (Gelug-pa)

The amazing monastery of Phuktal clings on to the side of a near-vertical cliff face, an apparition of unworldly mystery before the eyes. It is believed to date back to the 12th century and houses around forty monks. There is no road access and the trek to this shrine will take three to four days from Padum. This cave monastery edifice belongs to the yellow hat Gelug-pa sect. In the cave is a chorten, which is believed to contain the remains of the founding lama, Tserap Zangpo, who is also linked to Alchi and Likir.

Zongkul (Druk-pa Kagyu-pa)

Located just before the climb to the Omasi Pass begins, this is another spectacular cave monastery. Like a bird's nest, it clings improbably to the rock face. Naropa is believed to have meditated here, and his footprint is seen on a stone at the entrance to the lower cave. The excellent frescoes inside the cave are credited to the scholar-painter Zhadpa Dorje, who studied and worked here three hundred years ago.

Hanle Monastery

The Hanle Monastery is almost out of Ladakh, being well to the southeast of Zanskar closer to Spiti. It is located in the region known as the Chang Tang. Hanle is a large imposing fortress-like monastery, set high overlooking the surrounding barren landscapes.

Chapter Twelve

GENERAL INFORMATION

Visas

All foreigners require a visa to visit India. This must normally be obtained outside the country. Visas are issued on arrival at the airport in Delhi, and a few other Indian cities for certain nationalities – but be sure to double-check, as things are always changing. Visas issued 'abroad' are normally issued for six months multiple entry, but make sure you check with your local embassy for the latest information.

Money

These days' traveller's cheques are virtually extinct, so take a reasonable amount of your money in cash. ATMs can be found in most major places. Out in the Ladakhi countryside there is nowhere to change money, so make sure you get sufficient in Delhi or Leh.

Health

Malaria is a risk in other parts of India, but not in Ladakh. However, since most visitors travel to Leh during the summer months from parts of India where malaria is present, you should ask your doctor for the latest prevention and treatment advice before you leave home.

Although India is fast developing, health and hygiene are not up to Western standards and visitors should take care about what and where they eat. Do not eat unpeeled fruit or salads. Take care not to get dehydrated if you do get diarrhoea. There are pharmacies and a hospital in Leh.

Altitude

Flying into Leh will present the visitor with a breathtaking shock, as the altitude is 3505m. The first day should be spent relaxing and drinking tea, soft drinks or safe water. Do not overexert yourself! Headaches may be expected, which can be treated with painkillers if necessary. We personally have found homeopathic coca tablets to be a great help at altitude. Walking slowly up the numerous steps to most monasteries may be necessary at first, and stopping to take photographs is always a good excuse for a rest! Keep drinking lots of water to help acclimatisation.

What to take
Whenever you may visit Ladakh it can be cold, even in summer if it's cloudy and when the sun goes down. In spring and autumn it could snow heavily and in winter it is bitterly cold. A good sleeping bag is essential when staying in budget guesthouses. Warm clothing should be taken and walking boots if you plan a lot of exploring.

Getting to Ladakh
The fastest way is to take the 50-minute direct flight from Delhi. Both Jet Airways and Air India have early morning flights to Leh. Some Indian Airlines flights are routed via Jammu or Chandigarh. Other flights go to Srinagar in the Kashmir valley. Check about the latest security situation before committing to this route. In winter, October to May, Ladakh can only be reached by air.

Road routes open some time in May. Two routes exist. The usual and safer one is via Manali, Rohtang pass, Baralacha pass and into the Indus valley from the southeast. This route may take three or four days from Delhi. The older traditional route was from Srinagar over the Zoji La pass to Dras and then to Kargil and Leh. Currently security concerns may make this hazardous. The bus from Srinagar to Leh takes two days.

Getting around Ladakh
There are three possibilities: private taxi, public bus or walking. Taxis are expensive but prices are fixed by the municipality. Ask to see the driver's list if you are unsure. Taking a taxi will mean you don't have to wait around while the bus fills up, and you will be to get out without pushing your way through the crowds on the bus. A local bus, on the other hand, will give you more experience of how the local people live. Walking is only practical for monasteries close to Leh, or if you are taking

a public bus and then walking. Or if you find your road is blocked by snow and you are forced to walk, as we had to do to visit Rizong in January!

Another possibility might be to join a group excursion locally if the tour operators are willing.

Where to stay
Accommodation near outlying monasteries is given in the relevant chapters. Most visitors will stay in Leh and take day trips out from there. This section therefore lists hotels and guesthouses in Leh only. Expect some changes in the list as names change etc.

Close to Town
Hotel Lasermo – usually open in winter, friendly and helpful service and management; excellent food. Also Hotel Royal Palace, Hotel Kang La Chen, Hotel Yak Tail – open in winter, Meridian Hotel.

Hotel Shynam, Auspicious Guesthouse, Hotel Dreamland, Bijod Guesthouse, Pangong Guesthouse, Kongcho, Tso Mori, Indus Guesthouse.

West side of Leh and Changspa Area
Jigmet Guesthouse – open in winter, including heating. Millennium Guesthouse, Glacier View, Skylord, Dorje, Singey Guesthouse.

In Changspa
Omsila, Asia Guesthouse, Ortsel Guesthouse, Greenland, Sun n Sand, Ri-Rab Guesthouse, Lyon Guesthouse, Sonamchen Guesthouse, Namkela, Gobo Guesthouse.

Near Changspa Stupa
Gomang, Zeepata, Samba, Rai Wai, Solpon, Zec Guesthouse, Upper Changspa Guesthouse.

Map of Leh

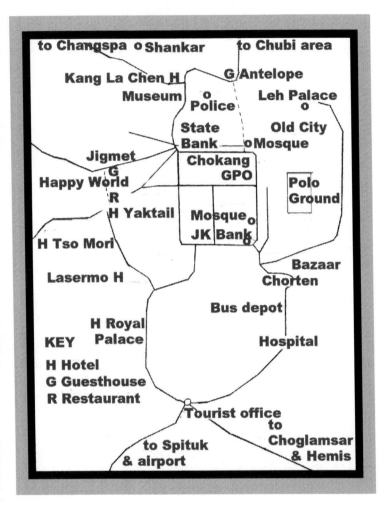

to Changspa o Shankar   to Chubi area

Kang La Chen H   G Antelope

Museum | o   Leh Palace

Police   o

State   Old City

Bank — o Mosque

Jigmet   Chokang

G   GPO

Happy World

R   Polo

H Yaktail   Ground

Mosque o

H Tso Mori   JK Bank

Lasermo H   Bazaar

Chorten

Bus depot

H Royal

KEY   Palace   Hospital

H Hotel

G Guesthouse

R Restaurant

Tourist office

to

to Spituk   Choglamsar

& airport   & Hemis

In Chubi

North of Antelope Guesthouse are: New Moon, Hotel Chube, Milarepa Guesthouse, Green Villa, Kunfan Guesthouse, Shashipa Guesthouse – open in winter, Ser Dung, Norbulingka, Phutsogling Guesthouse, Youthog Guesthouse, Katpa, Y Guesthouse, Rigyal, Mount View, Snow Lion, Onpo

Nor, Samala, Disket Village, Spoyba Guesthouse, Dongbog, Lamdotard, Arangol Guesthouse, Oriental Guesthouse – open in winter.

Eating Out

During the summer months, you can feast on the many different varieties of food said to be in Leh. But if you go in winter, take some emergency rations. Hotels do not like to serve outsiders, only those guests who are staying at their hotel, and even that does not always apply if you are staying in a small guesthouse. Hardly any restaurants or cafes are open, and those that are may close at 5.30pm! You have been warned!

Happy World café was always open and served delicious cheese naan. Other food served was a basic but tasty Indian vegetable curry, and packet tomato soup by special request.
Hotel Lasermo served excellent food if pre-arranged.
Amdo Tibetan restaurant in the main street was said to be open.
Hotel Yak Tail would only serve in-house guests.

Leh market seller

Appendices

APPENDIX 1: GLOSSARY

If you are a teacher, try not to merely transmit knowledge, but try at the same time to awaken your students' minds to basic human qualities such as kindness, compassion, forgiveness and understanding. Do not communicate these as though they were the reserve of ethics or religion. Show them that these qualities are indispensable for the happiness and survival of everyone.
Dalai Lama: *Daily Advice from the Heart*

apsara goddess or celestial nymph, usually seen dancing.
arhat a being who has managed to become free from the cycle of existence which is called 'samsara'. Arhats are not often seen as icons, but when they are, their faces have moustaches and beards. The sixteen arhats are the original disciples of Buddha.

bangrim the steps of a stupa.
Bardo the intermediate state between life and death; considered to be of forty-nine days' duration, before the soul finds a new body in which to be reincarnated.
bharal species of blue sheep.
bindu the very top of a stupa.
Bon pre-Buddhist religion of Tibet.
bumpa the dome of a stupa.

Cham dances performed by monks during festivals; religious dance/dramas with colourful costumes and masks.
chang home-brewed barley wine/beer, sometimes made with other grain.
charnel ground sky burial site.
chorten similar in shape to a small stupa; they do not normally contain relics. They are mostly found in high Buddhist

mountain country. Chortens are seen in profusion across Ladakh.

chu river.

chuba Tibetan national dress.

dharma the teachings of Buddhism as a whole; the path to enlightenment; a way of alleviating suffering.

dorje or vajra the thunderbolt. It destroys ignorance. It is a metal object found at many temples and shrines. It is the symbol of Indra, and in Tantra it is the male principle.

drubchu sacred spring.

drubkhang hermitage for meditation.

dukhang the main assembly hall of the monastery, where monks collectively come to offer prayer and meditation.

dZi long Tibetan bead, brown or black with white markings, worn around the neck in combination with turquoise and/or coral. Said to be 'precious jewels of supernatural origin', they are found underground and are considered to have come from the gods. Some are considered so valuable that their owners will not sell them for any amount of money. Geologically it is etched agate or banded chalcedony.

Dzogchen means literally 'Great Perfection'; a form of meditation of the Nyingma-pa and Kagyu-pa, practised to seek a 'a direct realisation of the nature of the mind'

dzong fortress, castle

eight auspicious symbols umbrella, fish, conch shell, eternal knot, vase, wheel, victory banner and flower.

ghaou the turquoise star necklace worn by women at their wedding ceremony, often around 25cm in diameter.

gonkhang a smaller chamber devoted to the protecting deities. Often dark and somewhat forbidding, this room may well house the images of Yamantaka, Mahakala and Palden Lhamo, among others.

harmika the square part of a stupa, between the dome and the spire. Often has eyes painted on it.

Hinayana the small vehicle of Buddhism, in which one is concerned with one's own liberation alone, and not that of the greater world of all sentient beings.

incarnation human form taken by a lama after a previous human life has ended.

Kalachakra initiation participants can gain help in liberation from suffering. Teacher and student alike seek peace of mind, using mantras, yoga and meditations.
Kangyur the part of the Buddhist 'Bible' containing the teachings of Buddha Sakyamuni. Thought to have been compiled by Buton Rinchendrub.
Kham the eastern part of Tibet, from where the current Dalai Lama comes.
khang house or building, sometimes used as an abbreviation of Lhakhang.
khyang Asiatic wild ass (Equus hemionus Pallas).
kira waistband worn with Chuba Tibetan national dress.
kumbum a stupa containing many thousands of images.

la mountain pass.
lama (guru in Sanskrit) a religious teacher and guide. Can be male or female. Very few monks and even fewer nuns are considered to be lamas.
lha spirit.
lhakhang temple within a monastery.
Losar Tibetan new year festival.

Mahayana the greater vehicle of Buddhism. Practitioners are dedicated to serving the welfare of all sentient beings, not only themselves.
mandala in art, this is a circular pattern made of many colours, often a square or squares within a circle. Represents 'the divine abode of an enlightened being visualised during Tantric practices.'
mani stone a (usually large) rock covered with engraved Buddhist mantras, sometimes painted.
mani wall a long wall made of flat stones with Buddhist mantras engraved on them. May also contain prayer wheels. You should always walk past one of the these walls clockwise, i.e. with the wall on your right.
mantra a series of Sanskrit syllables, not always words with an absolute meaning. Chanting these sounds is thought to create particular effects in the minds of oneself and others.

mudra a hand position, indicating a particular attitude in a Buddha or bodhisattva.

naga a snake or serpent god.

pandit a learned person.
phurba the ritual dagger carried by Vajrakila.
Potala the Dalai Lama's palace in Lhasa.
prayer flag cotton flags in five colours on which are printed prayers. These flutter in the wind sending prayers direct to heaven. The colours represent the five elements: earth, fire, air, water, and ether.
prayer wheel a metal wheel engraved with Tibetan script and containing prayers. May either be large and fixed into a wall, or hand held and spun while walking. Either way, the action of spinning the wheel activates the prayers.
puja a ceremony offering prayers, usually for a specific purpose such as blessing a house, for example.

samsara is the cycle of birth, death and rebirth. Ordinary reality, an endless cycle of frustration and suffering, is the result of karma.
sangha the community of Buddhists; one of the 'three jewels' of Buddhism. Sometimes used to refer to only monks and nuns, it can also mean all Buddhist practitioners.
serdung a stupa containing relics and made of gold; normally contains the relics of a very great lama.
Shambhala the mythical land, thought to lie north of Tibet.
stupa a large monument, usually with a square base, a dome on top and a pointed spire on top of that. The spire on top represents the levels towards enlightenment. A stupa might host the remains of a revered lama or teacher. In this case they are called reliquary stupas, as they contain the 'relics' or bones, and sometimes precious items, used by the deceased. Walking round a stupa in a clockwise direction is thought to bring great merit
sutra a teaching of Sakyamuni Buddha. The Kangyur is made up of a collection of these texts. These are the exoteric teachings of Buddha, as opposed to the esoteric teachings of the Tantras.

tangka see thangka.

171

Tangyur The part of the Buddhist 'bible' which contains Indian treatises or commentaries on the Buddha's teachings, as opposed to the Kangyur, made up of tantras and sutras, Buddha's own teachings. Thought to have been compiled by Buton Rinchendrub.

tantra Oral teachings and Buddhist scriptures forming part of the Kangyur, describing the use of mantras, mandalas and deities in meditation, and yoga for rechanelling bodily energies. The four classes of Tantra are: kriya (action), charya (performance), yoga and supreme yoga. The word is commonly associated with physical sexual methods of striving for enlightenment, but is equally applicable to meditation methods using the energies of the mind.

tathagata Another name for a fully enlightened Buddha. Literally translated, it means 'One who has gone thus'.

terma texts and sacred objects hidden in safe places on the Tibetan plateau during the time of Padma Sambhava, to be discovered at a later auspicious date by the tertons.

terton a person who discovered Padma Sambhava's hidden texts in Tibet during the early years of Buddhism's dissemination there.

thangka or **tangka** a religious painting, usually on silk fabric. Seen in all monasteries hanging on the walls or pillars.

torma a cake made of tsampa, butter and sugar. Used as an offering during religious ceremonies

tsampa roasted barley; the Tibetan staple food. Mixed with butter tea, it is made into a sort of porridge and eaten with the fingers.

tsa-tsa small shapes made of clay, usually mixed with relics or sacred items. Often made of the ashes of deceased lamas and placed inside reliquary stupas.

tulku an incarnate lama.

Tushita often referred to as Tushita heaven; the place where the future Buddha Maitreya now lives.

vajra see dorje.

vihara a large Buddhist temple.

yab-yum the depiction of two deities, male and female, in sexual union. Literally it means father-mother. The male represents compassion and the female wisdom. Deities found in this position depict not just a physical union, but the spiritual union that reaches to the pinnacle of awareness. This joining brings about a transformation of the fires and energies of passion to give everlasting long life.

yidam a tutelary deity; the deity with whom a Tantric practitioner feels a special affinity or closeness, and whom he/she visualises in meditation

yogi an advanced practitioner of Tantric meditation; male

yogini an advanced practitioner of Tantric meditation; female

Yoghurt festival an end of summer festival held in Lhasa on the 29th day of the 6th month

zi see dZi.

Zimchung is the head lama's chamber, often on the roof area.

See also *Significant Tibetan Buddhist Deities*.

Typical Ladakhi clothing

APPENDIX 2: BIBLIOGRAPHY

Ahmed, Monisha and **Harris**, Clare ed. by *Ladakh Culture at the Crossroads* Marg Publications Mumbai, 2005

Allen, Charles *A Mountain in Tibet* 1982

Allen, Charles *The Search for Shangrila* Little, Brown and Company, London 1999

Batchelor, Stephen *The Tibet Guide* Wisdom Publications Inc., USA, 1998

Baumann, Bruno *Kristalspiegel – Pilgerreise zum heiligen Berg – Kailash* Published by Nymphenburger, Munich 2005

Baumer, Christoph *Tibet's Ancient Religion, Bön* Orchid Press, Thailand, 2002

Bell, Charles *The People of Tibet* Clarendon Press 1928 reprinted by Book Faith India 1998

Chan, Victor *Tibet Handbook* Moon Publications 1994

Cunningham, Alexander *Ladak, Physical, Statistical and Historical* 1853 reprinted by Pilgrims 2005

Dalai Lama *365 Daily Advice from the Heart* Harper Collins, India

Dalai Lama *An Introduction to Buddhism and Tantric Meditation* Paljor Publications 1996

Dorje, Gyurme *Tibet* Footprint Handbooks 2004

Francke, Rev. A. H. *A History of Western Tibet* 1907 reprinted by Pilgrims 1998

Genoud, Charles and **Inoue**, Takao *Buddhist Wall Painting of Ladakh* Editions Olizane Geneva 1981

Gibbons, Bob & **Pritchard-Jones**, Siân *Kathmandu - Valley of the Green-Eyed Yellow Idol* Pilgrims 2004

Glasenapp, Helmuth Von *Jainism, an Indian religion of Salvation* Motilal Banarsidass Publishers Pvt. Ltd., Delhi, 1999 (reprinted from original 1925 edition)

Gordon, Antoinette *The Iconography of Tibetan Lamaism* Munshi Ram M Delhi 1978

Govinda, Lama Anagarika *The Way of the White Clouds* Rider and Company, London 1966

Goyal, Somesh *Spiti, a Visual Journey* Arya Publishing, Delhi, 2000.

Hedin, Sven *A Conquest of Tibet* Book Faith India reprinted 1994

Johnson and **Moran,** Kerry *Kailas: On Pilgrimage to the Sacred Mountain of Tibet* Thames & Hudson

Kalsang, Ladrang *The Guardian Deities of Tibet* Winsome Books, India 2003

Kapur, Brigadier Teg Bahadur *Ladakh the Wonderland* Mittal Publications, Delhi

Kaul, Shridhar & Kaul, H. N. *Ladakh Through the Ages* Indus, Delhi

Pustak Bhandar, Nepal

Kawaguchi, Ekai *Three Years in Tibet* 1909

Khadro, Chagdud *P'howa Commentary* Pilgrims 2003

Khosla, Romi *Buddhist Monasteries in the Western Himalaya* Ratna

Kohn, Michael *The Shambhala Dictionary of Buddhism and Zen* Shambhala Boston 1991

Kucharski, Radek *Trekking in Ladakh* Cicerone Press 2012

Lama, Tsewang *Kailash Mandala: A Pilgrims Trekking Guide* Humla conservation and development association, Kathmandu, Nepal

Lhalungpa, Lobsang P. *The Life of Milarepa* Book Faith India 1997

Pal, Pradapaditya *On the Path to the Void* Marg Publications Mumbai 1996

Pal, Pradapaditya A *Buddhist Paradise: The Murals of Alchi* Visual Dharma Publications, Hong Kong 1982

Pallis, Marco *Peaks and Lamas* 1939 reprinted Book Faith India 1995

Pranavananda, Swami *Kailash Manasarovar* Delhi 1949

Pritchard-Jones, Siân & **Gibbons**, Bob *Kathmandu - Valley of the Green-Eyed Yellow Idol* Pilgrims 2004

Prophet, Elizabeth Clare *The Lost Years of Jesus* Book Faith India 1994

Rizvi, Janet *Ladakh, Crossroads of High Asia* Oxford University Press 1983

Roerich, George *Tibetan Paintings*

Roerich, Nicholas *Altai Himalaya* 1929; reprinted by Book Faith India 1996

Singh Jina, Prem *Some monasteries of the Drigung-pa order in Central Ladakh* Sri Satguru, Delhi 1999

Singh Jina, Prem *Religious History of Ladakh* Sri Satguru, Delhi 2001

Singh, Neetu D. J. & **Singh**, D. J. *Ladakh* Brubasi Printers, New Delhi 1994

Snellgrove, David *Buddhist Himalaya* Himalayan Booksellers 1995(Asia edition from 1957 edition by Bruno Cassirer)

Snelling, John *The Sacred Mountain* London 1983.

Stein, R. A. *Tibetan Civilisation* Faber and Faber 1972 London

Tchekhoff, Genevieve and **Comolli**, Yvan *Buddhist Sanctuaries of Ladakh* White Orchid books, Bangkok 1987

Thurman, Robert & **Wise**, Tad *Circling the Sacred Mountain* Bantam Books, USA 1999

Tucci, Giuseppe *Cave of a Thousand Buddhas* Pilgrims Varanasi

Tucci, Giuseppe & **Ghersi**, E. *Secrets of Tibet* Cosmo Publications India 1996 (Asia edition) © Genesis Publishing Pvt Ltd, 24B Ansari Rd, Daryaganj, New Delhi, India.

Tucci Giuseppe, *Transhimalaya* Nagel Publishers, Geneva 1973

Related Topics and Books published by Pilgrims

Pilgrims Publications has devoted a lot of time and energy to presenting books on the subject of spiritual growth by meditation, yoga, Tantra, religious paths and erotic art forms. Earlier related publications and topics are also listed below.

Gibbons, Bob and **Pritchard-Jones**, Siân *Erotic Art of the Kathmandu Valley*

Goodman, Jim *Nepalese Festivals*

Miller, Casper *Faith Healers of the Himalaya*

Santiago, Jo *Sacred Symbols of Buddhism*

Shakya, Min Bahadur *Princess Bhrikuti Devi*

About the authors

Bob Gibbons and Siân Pritchard-Jones have been visiting Asia since 1974 and 1982 respectively. They have returned each year to Kathmandu, previously to lead treks in Nepal, drive overland tours across India or Asia and recently to write guidebooks to the greater Himalayan region.

Their first venture with Pilgrims was the publication of a trekking guide to Mustang and one to Tibet, also translated into French. A cultural guide to the Kathmandu Valley **Kathmandu:** *Valley of the Green-Eyed Yellow Idol* and introductory guides to Boudhanath and Swayambhunath soon followed.

They have also travelled extensively in and across Africa, and have written the fourth, fifth and sixth editions of the Bradt travel guide *Africa Overland*. For the same publisher, they have updated guides to the exotic isles of the Maldives in the Indian Ocean, and Cape Verde off the coast of West Africa.

In series with this book is their *Kailash and Guge: Land of the Tantric Mountain*. Covering the holy Mount Kailash in Tibet, its monasteries (including Tsaparang) are closely related to some of those in this book, since both areas were part of with the Guge kingdom seven hundred years ago.

Much more recently they have produced a series of trekking guidebooks to the Himalayan region of Nepal and Tibet. Titles published by Cicerone (UK) are *Mount Kailash* and *Annapurna*. In addition, for Himalayan Map House, the *Himalayan Travel Guides* series of trekking guidebooks covers Manaslu & Tsum Valley, Dolpo, Ganesh Himal, Everest, and the Langtang/Gosainkund/Helambu areas.

Siân and Bob at Mount Kailash

Dal Lake Houseboats, Srinagar

Notes:

Printed in Great Britain
by Amazon.co.uk, Ltd.,
Marston Gate.